SOLD FOR SEX

Sold for Sex

June Kane

arena

Published by
Arena
Ashgate Publishing Limited
Gower House
Croft Road
Aldershot
Hants GU11 3HR
England

Ashgate Publishing Company
Old Post Road
Brookfield
Vermont 05036
USA

British Library Cataloguing in Publication Data
Kane, June
    Sold for sex
    1. Exploitation 2. Children and sex 3. Child sexual abuse
    I. Title
    362.7'6

Library of Congress Cataloging-in-Publication Data
Kane, June
    [Chasse à l'enfant. English]
    Sold for sex / June Kane.
        p.   cm.
    Appeared in February 1997, in Paris, with the title: Chasse à l'enfant
    ISBN 1-85742-435-2 (pbk.)
    1. Child sexual abuse. 2. Sexually abused children. 3. Child
    molesters. 4. Child prostitution. 5. Children's rights.
    I. Title.
    HV6570.K36   1998
    362.76—dc21   97-42341
                                                            CIP

ISBN: 1-85742-435-2 (paperback)
ISBN: 1-85742-438-7 (hardback)

Typeset in Palatino by Raven Typesetters, Chester and printed and bound in Great Britain by Biddles Ltd, Guildford, Surrey.

Contents

Preface to the English edition

This book first appeared in February 1997, in Paris, with the title *Chasse à l'enfant*, or 'Hunt the Child'. The title came from a verse by the French poet Jacques Prévert, and seemed appropriate in a country where the sexual exploitation of children has traditionally occupied a small and controversial niche almost as a literary genre. We needed a new title for the updated, expanded English edition, but friends and colleagues have been surprised that it should be called *Sold for Sex*. 'The children are not always sold,' they say. 'What about little kids in Europe who are pulled into a back alley and violated, and then dumped? No money has changed hands. They have been used for sex, but they haven't been sold.'

Oh yes, they have. They have been *sold out*. We, all of us, have sold their souls in exchange for the freedoms we fought for and cherish but whose limits we have forgotten to set. The truth is that the majority of people who use children for sex are not 'paedophiles' in the true sense of the word; they are not psychiatrically inclined to seek out prepubescent children to fulfil their sexual fantasies. They are 'normal' people, men and sometimes women who use children for sex because they think it is OK to do so. From somewhere they have got the idea that sex with a 12-year-old is acceptable. More, that it's desirable. Fun, trendy, cool.

Now these are not the sexual freedoms that we fought for in the fifties and sixties. Maybe we did not realise, then, that we were fighting for those freedoms within a well-defined set of limits handed down from our parents, limits that we accepted and made our own. As a result, we gained sexual freedom but took on, too, the responsibility of setting our own personal, individual limits, and within these boundaries children were protected. For whatever reason, or reasons, it seems that the people who use children for sex have either not set such personal limits or have set them outside what most people – and, indeed, international law and conventions – consider acceptable. It is not surprising, then, that much of the debate that has surrounded

vii

the discussion of sexual exploitation of children in the past year has centred on whether and how societies should impose the limits that individual human beings seem reluctant or unable to define for themselves. This debate continues.

What fires the debate is the emotional weight of the subject. It is something that seems to touch each of us in one way or another. We have young children and fear for their safety. We remember an adult in our youth who was friendlier than we wanted. We know someone who went on holiday to an exotic country and brought back photos he couldn't show the wife. We pick up the paper and see stories of incidents that have been reported in the neighbourhood.

As an Australian, I find it particularly tragic to read reports of young Australian men who, often blessed with good looks, enough money to travel, and coming from a country where beauty and opportunity are easier to find than in most of the world, nevertheless go on holiday to Asia and buy themselves a young child for sex or to take 'dirty' pictures with, 'for a laugh'. Of all the hundreds of documents I read through every month, of all the dozens of cases I study of children, intermediaries and clients every week, to learn more about this issue, I think these young men and others like them are the ones that anger me most. They are the ones who benefit from the freedoms we fought for, and yet who abuse them and risk losing them. I don't believe, despite what they do, that these young men are fundamentally evil. I don't even believe they are stupid. Tragically, maddeningly, I believe they simply don't *think.*

That was my first reason for writing this book. I would like to believe that people will read it and *stop and think.* Not only think, but consider their own views on sexuality and on children, and check or set their own limits. I continue to believe in the innate goodness of the overwhelming majority of people, and that the defining of individual, personal limits is a realistic start in the fight against sexual exploitation of children.

The second reason I wrote this book at this time is because, after more than a year working with journalists all over the world on this issue on behalf of the co-sponsors of the first World Congress against Commercial Sexual Exploitation of Children (Stockholm, August 1996), I began to fear that the massive media coverage of the issue and, in particular, reports following the so-called 'Dutroux case' in Belgium in July 1996, were somehow becoming both dispersed and at the same time too focused on paedophilia and Europe. In fact, what happened in Belgium in 1996 and what happens in Asia, for example, every day of the year, are inextricably linked. What links them is the fact that some people can look at a child and see him or her as nothing more than a piece of merchandise to be sold, used and then thrown away. Whether it happens within the context of a European trafficking ring where children are traded like stolen cars, or on a Bangkok street corner where children are just another tourist attraction, the story is essentially the same. It was to underline these links and paint a fuller picture that I wanted to write this book.

There was a third reason. For 18 months I had spent almost every waking hour reading, listening, thinking, learning about how children are used and abused for sexual gratification. I have had the good fortune, at the same time, to have met and worked with some of the most courageous and wonderful people you can imagine, who have not only dedicated themselves to the fight to stop this happening, but who have also from time to time succeeded. Nevertheless, this work takes its toll. There have been tears and uncertainties and sometimes too much anger and too much despair. I needed to do something too, and what I do is write.

This book, then, is my contribution to the fight.

June Kane
Geneva, July 1997

1 Surely it doesn't happen here? A tour of the global market in child sex

Julie Lejeune and Mélissa Russo. Daniel Handley. Rosario Baluyot. These are the children whose names we repeat with shame and disbelief. These are children who died because adults valued short-term sexual gratification above children's bodies, above their dignity, above their lives.

But there are others, millions of others, whose names we do not know. They are the faceless, nameless children who turn up in reports as statistics, lost in the columns of figures – at best only estimates – of young people under the age of 18 who every year are kidnapped, sold, coerced, forced by people or circumstance into the commercial sex market or other forms of sexual exploitation.

While we all stop and draw in our breath at the terrible fate of Julie and Mélissa, Daniel and Rosario, it is so much more difficult to respond to a list of numbers, even when – perhaps especially when – they reach into the many hundreds of thousands.

This lack of sentiment, this inability to identify with the suffering of millions of children in our world, however, is itself a characteristic of the commercial sexual exploitation of children. For children who are sold into sex lose their identity. They are stripped of humanity. They are traded and used as goods, no better than toys stacked on a supermarket shelf or, more often, sold off a grubby stall on a street corner. They become little more than chattels in an illicit trade that seems to be growing, spreading across the world on the back of global consumerism, breakdown of the family, greed, poverty and shifting moral values.

And our inability to respond, to feel outrage and to act, has meant that those who sell and buy children for sex have been able to go about their trade largely unchallenged, and to prosper. For too long we have preferred not to ask questions about men whose interest in young children seemed unusual, about children who have gone missing and have disappeared without a trace, about business colleagues and friends whose holiday photos of young

1

kids in sexy poses have caused a few raised eyebrows but nothing more, about advertising in our own local papers offering teenage sex, and about local corner stores who sensitively put the so-called 'soft' porn magazines featuring obviously under-age models on a high shelf so as not to offend the dignity of customers.

We have closed our eyes to the fact that, in almost every part of the world, children are being sold for sex.

But the days of blissful ignorance are over. In the words of Vitit Muntarbhorn, Thai professor of law and tireless campaigner for children's rights: 'there can be no more delusions'.[1] We have woken up to the unquestionable truth that there are people who sell our children to others who just want to use them for sex and then discard them. And we have begun to understand how it works, what lies behind it and – at last – how we can come together to fight it and maybe one day stop it.

Beginning in the brothels of Bangkok

Until the paedophile ring scandal that shocked Belgium in August 1996, most people who had heard about so-called 'child prostitutes' (a catch-all name for children trapped in the sex trade that belies the fact that most of them are there unwillingly and are therefore *prostituted*, rather than prostitutes) believed that children being sold for sex was something that happened only in Asia, and only in the poorer parts of Asia at that. The phenomenon was seen as something 'cultural', something to do with the sun, the exoticism of the East, some deep-rooted desire in the women of Asia, especially the younger ones, to please.

The truth is not so simple and, indeed, the phenomenon of commercial sexual exploitation of children is a highly complex web of root causes, historical developments, motivating factors, players and results.

In Asia, sexual exploitation of children is deep-rooted and widespread. It is, despite general perceptions, usually the girl child who is exploited, and mostly by local men. This is fundamental to the problem, because the place of the girl child in most Asian societies and, indeed, of the adult woman too, is at the bottom of the heap. There is a saying in Cambodia that 'women are cloth; men are gold'. There is no better way to sum up a society where the woman is essentially seen as a source of pleasure for the man and where men regularly visit prostitutes even after marriage. Women are expected to be subservient and to fulfil men's wishes. Surveys conducted amongst prostitutes in the Cambodian capital Phnom Penh[2] suggest that such is the dominance of men that the prostitutes regularly provide unprotected sex, even though they know that this leaves them and their clients open to diseases including HIV/AIDS, because they are too scared to ask the men to use condoms. The same survey shows that, when these men go home to their wives, even the educated wives are too scared to insist on condom use by husbands they know to be visiting prostitutes.

In short, in many Asian countries sex is seen as something that men have a right to, at will and according to their own rules. Women are there simply to provide the opportunity for men to dominate them and take their pleasure. There is also an element of what has been called 'otherness' involved: often the prostitutes (adult and child) are from 'out of town', potentially trafficked across the border from a neighbouring country or brought from other areas where the ethnic mix might be different and the people therefore 'foreign'. This 'otherness', it has been suggested, allows the men to throw off any sense of inappropriateness in their behaviour, and to tell themselves that the prostitute they visit is an inferior being, racially inclined to prostitution and therefore accepting and compliant.

This same patronising, self-serving racism also turns up in interviews with so-called 'sex tourists' from the west,[3] who often deny their identity as exploiters and reason, instead, that the woman (or child) somehow 'expected it' and that buying a child for sexual purposes is therefore little more than bowing to local custom, like taking off your shoes when you enter a holy place, or sampling the local food.

Imagine how much more 'macho' the man can feel if the 'opportunity' offered to him in the local brothel is under-age. And how much safer he can feel when the brothel owner assures him that the child is a virgin, untainted by the diseases the newspapers keep telling us about. Indeed, doesn't ancient wisdom tell us that sex with a child can invigorate an ageing man and even bring success in business? There is a long-held Chinese belief, which has currency in other parts of Asia too, that everything has yin (female) or yang (male) properties, and that deflowering a virgin child helps to bring these two cosmic forces into balance and so slows down the ageing process and brings luck. It takes little imagination and just a small desire to find an excuse for exploitative behaviour, to extend this ancient myth into a reason for seeking out young children for sex.

So it is that the fear of HIV/AIDS, the twisted interpretation of rejuvenating myths and the desire to dominate at all costs has led to younger and younger children, especially girls, being in demand in Asia.

In some parts of Asia, too, particularly Cambodia and Vietnam, this demand was fuelled by the presence of foreign military troops stationed in the country. Away from their home environments, freed from the limits imposed by civil society and personal morality, groups of men are known to indulge in activity that even they might consider 'forbidden' in other circumstances.[4] Thus it is that American and other troops stationed in Asia in the sixties and seventies drove up the demand for prostitutes, including minors, and helped create a market that was at first demand-driven and then, after the troops had gone home to their wives and girlfriends, supply-led. More-over, the sight of western men regularly visiting prostitutes and accepting young children as service-providers broke down any cultural taboos that might have existed against child exploitation, and opened the door to local men overtly seeking out minors in prostitution.

These same troops also took home with them stories of exotic women in strange-smelling beds, of young children ready to please on the beach, in a hut, in the backroom of a bar where the liquor was cheap and you never ran into anyone from home.

And so, along with the local men who gained strength from the foreigners' example, came overseas tourists seeking a new experience, something they could tell their mates about over a drink when they got home or that they could share more privately with like-minded abusers. These 'sex tourists' used to travel in packs, on specially organised trips where everything they might require was provided, from air transportation to hotel and meals, to 11-year-old girls to have sex with. Now more often than not the travellers are on their own, frightened away from the organised tours by the media investigations encouraged by the lobbying of non-governmental organisa-tions (NGOs) and campaigners like the group known as ECPAT (End Child Prostitution in Asian Tourism), which since 1990 has targeted sex tourists in Asia and has succeeded in bringing about law reform, better implementation of the laws and a number of well-publicised convictions.

In Asia, too, there has long been a tradition of the 'nice old gentleman' expatriate, who has settled in an Asian country after a spell working in the region and who hands out kindnesses to the families of the locality. In many ways, this 'kind uncle' is even more insidious, because he convinces the families – and himself – that he really cares for the children, that the money he hands over is for their education, for better food or to help the family. This blood money – for that is surely what it is – soothes his conscience and helps the family to turn a blind eye when 'uncle' asks for more than gratitude from the children.

Such was the case of 'Uncle Bill', according to a May 1996 edition of the Indonesian news magazine *Tiras*. William Stuart Brown had been an Australian diplomat to Indonesia and had regularly visited the Indonesian island of Lombok over a number of years. He set up a travel office on the island and was known as part of a group of five Australian men which included Robert 'Dolly' Dunn, a paedophile whose activities were well known.

Over a period of years, 'Uncle Bill' reportedly invited young boys from poor families to his house. There he gave them food and sweets, and some-times money ranging from Rp 5000 (£1.25) to Rp 100 000 (£27.50). According to reports in the 20 May 1996 issue of *Forum Keadilan*, another Indonesian magazine, the boys were then expected to perform oral and anal sex with the

Australian men. The Australians fled Indonesia after Australian Federal Police tipped off the Indonesian authorities. They left behind them more than 40 boys around the age of ten, including two brothers, 'Uncle Bill's' favourites, who are reported to be 'disturbed' and to have performed poorly in school as a result.

And so the vulnerable children of Asia – girls without power, children of both sexes without food and other basic necessities often looking for friendship, caring and a way to escape the poverty of their lives, sons and daughters of families who knowingly or unwittingly sell them into bondage to raise money sometimes to survive but sometimes to buy a much-prized consumer durable – can be caught in many different ways and end up providing sex to a variety of clients.

No matter how the children are enslaved, however, nor who sells or buys them, they face similar consequences from this dirty trade.

The health impacts of sexual exploitation on children are enormous. Young children's bodies are simply not ready for sex. They are fragile and tear easily, so that the children often suffer lesions, bleeding, massive scarring and, if the wounds are not treated – and they often are not – infection, sterility and sometimes death. And so much for the belief that children are less likely to transmit venereal diseases, including HIV/AIDS. Children are even more likely to become seropositive given not only their fragile bodies which damage so easily and membranes which are more porous than in an adult, but also their weakness and inability to insist on safe sex practices or to refuse multiple clients.

Once the children are infected they also face discrimination and rejection if they do manage to escape the sex trade. More often than not their families will not take them back, the community rejects them and their only chance of survival is returning to a pimp, brothel or street corner, where they become sicker and pass on to more customers the disease that is killing them.

Their mental health suffers, too, as they are introduced to sexual acts which they often cannot understand but which they may feel devalue their bodies and their souls. They become confused about their role in life, their sexuality and – in the case of children used by paedophiles who entice them with gifts and promises of affection – they come to distrust adults who offer them 'love' and then abuse and abandon them. It is not surprising, then, that so many children caught up in the sex trade stay in it and even feel compelled to return to it when they have been helped to escape. Or that too many cannot cope with life inside or outside the sex trade and try to harm themselves, sometimes ending the lives they can no longer bear to live.

This is just a snapshot of some of the forms commercial sexual exploitation of children takes in Asia and elsewhere. It is a gruesome picture. And it is little wonder that many of the children who face this awful fate also fall prey to alcohol and drugs. Often these are used to trap the child in the first place, and to keep them submissive while they are being exploited. Too often, also, the children themselves turn to alcohol and drugs to numb the indignity and pain they suffer. 'Sometimes you just have to swallow hard and drink another gin,' a prostituted teenager in Bangkok is quoted as saying in a *New York Times* article of January 1996.[5] 'I couldn't get through some nights unless I was drunk.'

In this same article, Andrew Vachss, a New York writer who is actively engaged in a controversial campaign to boycott goods made in Thailand as a personal crusade against sexual exploitation of children there, cites Thailand as 'certainly not the only country [where this happens], but the international symbol of this problem. It's a place', he says, 'where children are disposable, like Kleenex.'

Certainly the selling of children for sex is perhaps most visible in Bangkok, where a walk down any crowded street in the red light districts of Patpong and Lumphini Park will provide ample evidence that the much-vaunted moves by the Thai Government to enact laws protecting children from exploitation have had little impact so far.

The child sex trade in Thailand prospered in the years of the Vietnam War, when new legislation was introduced formalising the entertainment industry in an attempt to capture some of the lucrative 'Rest and Recreation' market servicing American troops in the region. Although prostitution had been criminalised in 1960, in a half-hearted attempt to sell the message that Thailand was a 'safe place' for right-thinking GIs to go for some peace and quiet to escape the fighting, it proliferated in the guise of massage parlours, escort agencies, discos, hotels, gas stations, go-go bars, tearooms, barber shops, beauty salons and cabarets. These laid on 'entertainment' for the servicemen on R&R in a form which was acceptable both to the American forces, who hardly wanted the folks back home to know what their men were doing out there in Asia, and to the Thai authorities happy to earn valuable foreign exchange under the guise of 'legitimate' service provision. As a result, 'gradually ad-hoc practices of hosting prostitution ... became systemic as a result of the high rate of capital accumulation'.[6] In other words, selling sex brought in the money.

The word soon got round that Thailand was a great place for cheap sex. 'Glory' movies about the Vietnam War perpetuated the image of silky-haired good-time girls; criminals looking to make quick money soon began organising so-called 'sex tours' to Thailand and, by 1980, of the 15.8 million tourists who visited Thailand, 73 per cent were men.[7]

The economic benefits of such 'sex tourism' have traditionally been substantial. It has provided foreign exchange and large profits for local entrepreneurs, travel companies in Thailand and overseas, tourist and leisure companies such as hotel chains and restaurants. When local demand is also taken into account, the sex trade sector is among the most lucrative income-earners for governments not only in Thailand but in other parts of the world too.

The growing trend towards children being sold into this sex trade to cope with increased demand, fear of disease and a generally devalued image of the child, caused a conflict of interests in governments around the region which for many years was most easily dealt with by ignoring or, worse, denying that it existed. It is only in very recent times, in the face of growing international outrage which might turn the tide of tourism and begin reversing the economic gains that it brings, that Asian governments in general have begun to speak out about the sexual exploitation of children and to target foreign nationals and bring them to justice in highly publicised court cases.

Despite some moves against commercial sexual exploitation of children in Thailand, however, estimates of the number of children who are sold for sex in that country still range from 100 000 (UNICEF) to 800 000 (Centre for the Protection of Children's Rights). ECPAT, which started its life as a campaign called 'End Child Prostitution in Asian Tourism'[8] and which is still based in Bangkok, has researched this issue since 1990, and estimates that there are some 250 000 prostitutes under the age of 18 in Thailand (which had a population in 1996 of 59 million).

One final shocking figure before we leave Thailand and continue our journey through Asia: in 1990 half a million people in Thailand were HIV-positive. By 1993 the number was rising by 1400 a day.[9]

Cambodia also witnessed a boom in prostitution and entertainment services for foreign troops when, in 1990 and 1991, soldiers of the United Nations Transitional Authority in Cambodia (UNTAC) arrived. Although prostitution in general and child exploitation in particular had been criminalised and firmly dealt with during the years of communist rule, subsequent liberalisation and rising economic development in Cambodia increased rather than discouraged the growing sex trade. So much so that one reporter has dubbed the Cambodian market in child sex one of 'Asia's plantations of the '90s'.[10]

A 1995 UNICEF report conservatively estimated that, of the 10 000 to 15 000 prostitutes working in Cambodia, one-third were under-age. Son Ma[11] was one of them.

> My family was in difficulty, so I asked my mother if I could live in my grandmother's house. My grandmother said that, if I lived with her, I would have no money to support my mother and so would have to go and sell beer. I sold beer for five months. I got to know a lady who I would never have expected to do something bad to me. She told me in Battambang I would earn much more money and that she would feed me. When I asked her if her words were true she replied that she was old and didn't tell lies. She said I had better go for the sake of my family and my future.

I spent one month thinking about that. Then I decided to leave Phnom Penh for Battambang . . . I was taken to a home which I was told was the home of a relative of the lady. They asked me to take a rest because I looked tired. Then the relative asked me to take a bath before having lunch. I followed her suggestion and changed my clothes. After speaking to the owner of the house and receiving money from her, the old lady told me to wait for her and not to worry because this was the house of a relative. Then she left . . .

The house owner asked me to dress and make up to receive the guests. I asked her why I should make up and for what. She said that the old lady had sold me to her for 5000 Baht [£115], that I had to pay her back by selling sex otherwise I would be beaten and sold to Aryanprathet or somewhere else. I didn't agree to entertain the guests. She whipped me with electric wire and wooden bars . . .

Son Ma was kept as a sex slave for five months before police raided the house and rescued her and two other young women. She was taken to a centre in Phnom Penh set up to receive children who escape exploitation and to help them to learn skills which will allow them to earn a living. Son Ma is training to become a hairdresser.[12] She is not yet 18 years old.

Her case is typical of the fate of most children sold into sex in Cambodia. They are taken away from their home town or community, often supposedly to a better life elsewhere, working in a shop or as a servant. Once away from familiar surroundings, they are on-sold to a brothel-owner or pimp who may sell them again. They may be sold again, so that eventually the family loses track of them. Thus they join the ranks of other exploited children trafficked across borders from Vietnam, Laos, Thailand, China and the Philippines. Far from their homes, these young women often do not even speak the language of their customers. Nor do they speak the language of the country, should they succeed in escaping. They cannot explain what has happened to them or ask for help. And they are illegal immigrants, without papers, and therefore 'criminals' in the eyes of the justice system, fit only to be imprisoned.

The price of a child in Cambodia is between £25 and £150, depending on the perceived beauty of the child. The brothel-owner can sell the children to clients for a week's 'service' for between £120 and £300 when they are still virgins. Many of the customers of such a 'prize' will be ethnic Chinese from Taiwan, China or Singapore. They have the money to spend. Once the child has been deflowered, the price falls substantially and local customers are more common.

Between 1990 and 1994, 50 children were rescued from brothels in Beantey Mean Chey province in Cambodia. The police did not take the brothel-owner to court but made him pay compensation to the children's parents and let him off with a warning. The children were back where they started: returned to a family situation which had forced them into slavery in the first place.

The police argued that there are no laws in Cambodia relating specifically to the sexual exploitation of children, yet Cambodia has ratified the United

Nations *Convention on the Rights of the Child*, the most widely ratified UN Convention of all time. Article 34 of the Convention calls upon signatories to 'protect the child from all forms of sexual exploitation and sexual abuse', in particular to prevent 'the inducement or coercion of a child to engage in any unlawful sexual activity; the exploitative use of children in prostitution or other unlawful sexual practices; the exploitative use of children in porno-graphic performances and materials'. Importantly, the Convention commits States Parties to review their laws, including those relating to child protection and the exploitation of children for sexual purposes, and to bring them into line with the aims of the Convention. In August 1996, however, Cambodia's representative to the first World Congress against Commercial Sexual Exploitation of Children (called from here on 'the Stockholm Congress') described his government's efforts as 'still quite limited and inadequate, given the magnitude of the problem. Nevertheless,' he said, 'this is a begin-ning.'

Cambodia has a long, long way to go. Lurking around the corner, for example, are the western sex tourists who have 'done' Thailand and are look-ing for new adventures. They have already been advised about alternatives: 'If you're looking for an adventure,' they can read on the World Sex Guide site on the Internet, 'Cambodia is IT right now.' It has been pointed out, though, that 'a few foreign paedophiles do not sustain an industry; it needs a large domestic client base, corrupt and ineffective law enforcement, and an ample supply of parents desperate enough to sell their children'.[13]

There are plenty of those in many parts of Asia. But poverty alone does not push families to sell their children into the sex trade. There are countless families living in abject poverty who would rather die than see their children suffer this fate. What, then, pushes a family to sell a child?

Leonilla Olayres found a reason. She is a 33-year-old mother in the Philippine capital, Manila. She has several children, including two daughters aged ten and 12. She also has a karaoke machine in the corner of her home, paid for with the money she got for selling the girls to a Japanese man who supposedly wanted to take photos of them. He wanted much more of the ten-year-old, whom he tied to the bed and forced to perform oral sex. He gave her mother US$60 (£36) for the privilege.

The Philippine police put the man in jail. In early 1996, the Philippines House of Representatives passed a bill calling for the death penalty in certain cases of paedophilia. The bill defines paedophilia as a 'psycho-sexual perver-sion' and prescribes the death penalty if a child under 15 dies or becomes insane as a result of sexual acts. Convictions which do not meet these criteria can, in any case, attract life imprisonment.

It is astounding that, in one region of the world, the punishment for commercial sexual exploitation of children ranges from death to being let off with a warning. It is not surprising that criminals who trade in the dignity and lives of children find it safer at times to ship them across borders. This way not only are they able to move across legal jurisdictions, they are also less likely to be caught, as the serial sale of the children covers their tracks. The children themselves are plunged deeper and deeper into the sex market, growing ever more vulnerable as they find themselves in strange places where they do not speak the language and have no way of seeking help.

Asian children are trafficked from country area to big city, from village to town, from Vietnam to Thailand, across the Mekong from Laos into neighbouring countries, from Burma to Thailand and Pacific Rim countries and, in the South of Asia, from Nepal to India.

In the brothels of Bombay, the fair-skinned girls from Nepal are particularly prized. In 1996 estimates of Nepalese minors prostituted in the cities of India ranged from 30 000 to 200 000. Between 5000 and 7000 are trafficked every year. That same year, 400 girls were lost from one village, Gyanghapedi, alone. The pattern follows much the same as that in the countries of the Mekong: deception, the promise of a better life for a family living in poverty, sale or abduction, bondage and slave labour, brutal treatment and little hope of escape. But one set of statistics stands out in reports on trafficking between Nepal and India: doctors in India report that 70 per cent of the Nepalese children prostituted in India are HIV-positive.[14]

Maya is one of them. She was rescued with 129 other children from the red-light districts of Bombay by a Nepalese social organisation and with the help of the Government of Maharashtra state.[15] She had been working there since she was nine years old. Once diagnosed as seropositive, like the majority of those who become ill and are no longer 'useful' to the brothel-keepers and pimps, she was sent back to Nepal. Her family, which she had supported with the meagre money she was given by the people who sold her, refused to take her back and she was taken into care by one of several community-based organisations which provide homes for girls rescued from Indian brothels. There she told a reporter for *India Today*, 'I want to forget my past.'[16] No-one had yet told her that she would have a very short future.

The story of Maya is repeated in countries throughout the Asian continent. Between 20 000 and 40 000 children are in prostitution in Pakistan, 100 000 in India's major cities, more than a quarter of a million reported in China – where the true magnitude of the problem can only be guessed at – and up to 60 000 in Taiwan. Another quarter of a million in Thailand, according to non-governmental organisations, 20 000 to 30 000 in Sri Lanka. Ten thousand in Bangladesh, 40 000 in Vietnam, 42 000 in Indonesia, anything between 60 000 and 600 000 in the Philippines. The zeros stretch into infinity, like the suffering of the children and the limitless demand of sex-hungry customers who simply do not care if the vessel they are pumping into is a child to whom the world has promised play, learning, freedom and a future with dignity.

'By our estimates there will be tonight upwards of a million children in Asia alone who will spend the evening providing sexual services for adults,' ECPAT Co-ordinator Ron O'Grady told delegates at the opening of the Stockholm Congress in August 1996. 'If our surveys are correct they will receive 10 to 12 million adult male customers during the week we are in Stockholm.'

And so the images of child sexual exploitation in Asia which colour our nightmares are of frightened girls taken from their homes to be smuggled across borders to imprisonment in filthy cubicles where they are raped, beaten and burned by local and foreign men, or of sad-eyed boys in incongruously luxurious homes servicing the lust of western paedophiles.

The picture of children sexually exploited in South America is in some ways quite different. Here the nightmare is not played out against a background of exotic oriental music from the bars and nightclubs, or the laughter and shouts of people playing on the sands of crowded beaches. It is punctuated by the cacophonous klaxons of passing taxis and cars, and by the silence of back alleys where drugs are snorted and injected.

For most of what we know about the child sex trade in South America has come from those who work with street children.

Stop-over on the streets of South America

Many of the children who live and work on the streets of South America have arrived there from homes in which they have been sexually abused, or are escaping from families which threw them out as one too many mouth to feed. On the streets they have to work to survive. Already they are among the world's most vulnerable; they have already lost the very things that the *Convention on the Rights of the Child* aims to guarantee for all children: education, health, a stable family, recreation, a childhood.

They work as shoe-shine boys, flower sellers, car windscreen cleaners, hawkers. For long days they struggle to earn enough to eat. They are ripe for the picking. All too soon pimps will move in on them, offering them an 'easier' way to earn more money. Or they will come face to face with drug dealers who use them as messengers, pay them in crack cocaine and then exploit them once they are hooked on the drug. Sometimes they will give in to circumstance and offer themselves for sex, aware that they can make more in one night of sex than they might make in a week selling the goods they value as much as their own bodies.

'Poverty is a well spring from which child prostitution grows and expands,' argues Dorianne Beyer of the NGO Defence for Children International, noting also that many of the girls working in prostitution on the streets of South America have run away from family violence and incest.

On the streets of Fortaleza, a city on the beautiful north-east coast of Brazil, there are 15 000 abandoned children and teenagers, among them at least 2000 sexually exploited children. There is almost no industry in Fortaleza, so the children sell knick-knacks on the street corners, although their livelihood is now threatened by the competition of smuggled small goods from Paraguay.

But there are plenty of tourists. And with the tourists, a thriving trade in drugs and under-age prostitution. And there are mafia groups, black market money dealers, pimps, taxicab drivers, local businessmen, hotel and motel managers, bar owners – a veritable brick wall of criminals closing in the children whose vulnerability leaves them open to exploitation.

Some of the children think they can see a gap in the wall.

Luciana is 17 years old and has met the man of her dreams, her 'Prince Charming'. He is an Italian who has been showering her with gifts and has even given her parents a television set so that she will be allowed to go back to Italy and marry him. A new life awaits her.

She will undoubtedly find that the new life is not too different from her old life, except that she will not understand the language of her exploiters. Her story is familiar to Sister Elisabeth, a nun who works for the Casa Mae in Fortaleza. She invites street girls like Luciana to the Casa to talk, so that they can learn what it means to accept a foreigner's invitation to 'go and live overseas'. Sister Elisabeth knows that most of the girls will simply be trafficked into European brothels, and she warns them of this, gives them advice on how to look after their health, and encourages them to sign up for courses which might offer them an alternative way to survive, in typing and sewing. But Sister Elisabeth also knows her words often fall on barren ground. Most of the girls who have worked as prostitutes know their marriage prospects have been destroyed and so it is worth taking the chance that their Prince Charming might mean what he says.[17]

The children selling sex on the streets of Fortaleza are not all street children. Many of them, in fact, come from middle-class families, who know what they are doing and turn a blind eye to this horrific way of earning extra pocket-money. Substance abuse plays a large part in this, as both children and their parents need money to pay for the freely available drugs. These children are often described as selling sex 'voluntarily', when in fact they are compelled by addiction or the pressures of consumer society to get money one way or another.

Increasingly the children selling sex on the streets of Fortaleza are younger. A 1996 report showed that some 20 per cent were 15 or 16; 31 per cent were 13 or 14; 30 per cent were 11 or 12; 17 per cent were between eight and ten and more than 1 per cent were younger still.[18]

Foreigners and Brazilians from the big cities travelling on so-called 'sex tours' are not the only customers these children have to service. The north of

Brazil has the dubious honour of presenting the 'most varied sexual exploitation of children' reported.[19]

Many of the children will be shipped out to service the men of the mining towns of Amazonia. These regions, known as 'garimpos', house some 150 000 people, most of whom are men known as 'garimpeiros' working in the gold mines. As always in areas where there are large groups of unaccompanied men, there is a thriving entertainment sector, with bars and clubs offering 14-year-olds for sex on the menu.

The children are lured there with the promise of work in the canteens, earning more money than they could dream of in the city. They are offered transportation, but there is something they are not told: they will have to repay their air ticket before they start to receive any money. They also have to pay for lodging, clothes, food. They never pay off the debt. Instead, they are forced to sell themselves and are traded from one brothel to another, as the regular clients get sick of bedding the same child.

Flight is impossible. The region is isolated and the mine-owners set the rules. One 12-year-old girl who refused one night to take her twelfth customer (the girls are regularly expected to service ten to 15 men a day) was decapitated.[20] Others have been washed up in the river.

On the streets of the cities, the beaches of the northern coast, the mining towns of Amazonia, the sexually exploited children of Brazil number some half a million.

They share the same fate as children in Chile, where there is a strong connection between commercial sexual exploitation of children and the drug trade, and in Peru, where half a million children under 14 live in poverty and many enter the sex trade just to survive. Civil disruption in Colombia was largely behind a reported 500 per cent increase in sexual exploitation of children between the ages of eight and 13 in the seven years from 1986 to 1993, although the uneven distribution of wealth and drug dependency are major factors too. There are reported to be 5000 children working as prostitutes on the streets of the Colombian capital, Bogota, alone.

Argentina, Cuba, the Dominican Republic, Venezuela and Ecuador also have well-documented child sex trades, with thriving sex tourism sectors. The foreign exploiters who travel to these countries often do not distinguish between an adult prostitute and an exploited child. And the tourism industry is so important that most governments, as in Asia, prefer to leave well alone.

Costa Rica is a good example. Following a fall in coffee prices in 1978 and a rise in oil prices the next year, Costa Rica's economy slumped. By 1981, it owed US$4 billion in foreign debt and had to suspend repayments on international loans. In an attempt to bring in hard currency, the government targeted the tourist industry as a prime growth sector. By 1992, Costa Rica was winning awards for ecologically responsible tourism.[21]

Along with the 'eco-tourists', however, came large numbers of dedicated

North American and European sex tourists, as well as groups of male tourists who, while ostensibly visiting for the water sports and just for a good time in this beautiful country, also indulge in a little holiday sex, rarely stopping to ask the age of the object of their lust.

It is almost impossible to say how many children are caught up in sex tourism in Costa Rica. Many adults and children work in the sex trade temporarily to be able to eat – so-called 'survival sex' – and so the data can vary as much as the seasons. Figures for San José alone, though, give some idea of the size of the problem. There are more than 300 brothels in San José, with an average of ten women and children working in each. This would suggest that some 3000 women and girls are formally employed as prostitutes in a city of only 278 373 people – 1.1 per cent of the entire population prostituted in brothels. And this is of the entire population. If the percentage were calculated on the basis of just women and girls between the ages of 15 and 30, it would be much higher.

Outside this formal sector, there are large numbers of 'informal' sex workers, including many under-age children. Among these are drug-addicted children as young as eight, who sell their bodies for less than US$2.50 (£1.50) a time. These 'freelancers' generally work out of bars which charge an entrance fee and high prices for drinks and food. Both the freelancers and the brothel-workers are known as 'putas', and are distinguished from 'zorras', which refers to girls and women who enter into less explicitly sexual arrangements with tourists, for example as 'guides' and 'girl companions'.

To the bars flock the Filipino, Japanese and Argentinian sailors as well as local men. Perpetuating the myth that 'men need sex', these clients rarely ask the age of the girl lying on the bed. They simply do not care. They 'need' sex and that is what counts.

The local men, in particular, see their sexual urges as 'natural and inevitable' and look only to have them serviced. The heady Catholicism of the country reinforces this, so that the men make a clear distinction between 'madonnas' whom they will marry and who will bear their legal offspring, and 'whores' who are no more than a means to satisfy their natural macho needs.

The bars also attract sex tourists from Europe and North America.

The sex tourists also like the 'zorras' concept. It allows them to think they are not using prostitutes at all, but rather making friends, becoming part of the local scene, building up real relationships with girls and young women who are not, after all, in the sex trade but might just want to have sex with them after they have become friends. They share this fantasy with many of the more than 30 000 Americans and Canadians who have retired to Costa Rica. Large numbers of these are known as 'sexpats': expatriates who have retired to Costa Rica to enjoy the climate, the tax advantages, the low cost of living and the cheap and easily available sex.

Bob is one of these. He is in his early sixties and retired from the US Navy.[22] An unlikely contender for honours in any sexual race back home in the United States, he is flattered, overwhelmed by the fact that in Costa Rica the young women seem to enjoy sex with him. He fools himself into thinking that the young girls offered to him by men he meets really do like him, that they are not in the sex trade but need money to support their families, that in any case the youngest children in this paradise are sexually active by nature. Bob has bought into the myth of the 'noble savage' who follows instincts, has no inhibitions and exudes generosity of spirit and body. He is typical of sex tourists who rationalise their exploitation of children by claiming that sex is 'normal' for children in these countries. 'They all get pregnant by the age of 13,' a 52-year-old Canadian told Julia O'Connell Davidson. 'This is such an open, natural culture. Girls are so willing and open, they want to please. They're sexual from the age of six...'

Incredibly, the word 'natural' punctuates their justifications in the same way that the word 'pervert' is dotted through the judgements of those who read about them. O'Connell Davidson sums it up: 'the sexual exploitation of young girls is simply part of the natural order of things [in their eyes]: naturally, they use their sexuality to do this; naturally, adult men want to fuck 13-year-old girls; and naturally, the girls enjoy it'.

Many men like Bob and the Canadian also advertise in local English language newspapers for girlfriends or even wives. Many of the advertisements, however, lead respondents into the clutches of paedophile rings like those which work in the beach resorts of Asia: retired men or paedophiles who have set up small businesses as a base for their networks. They infiltrate the community, getting to know families and children and those already exploited into the sex trade. They lure them to their homes with promises of money, favours and friendship. There they often show the children pornographic videos or pictures, first of all 'for a giggle' and then, as the pornography gets harder, as an enticement to play out the same roles.

Making movies out of misery

It is worth stopping here for a moment to look at the role of pornography in the sexual exploitation of children, for so many people look upon it as 'harmless' and wonder why those who work with children who have been raped, tortured, infected and discarded should make so much fuss about a little videocassette or an envelope stuffed with 'dirty pictures'.

To understand exactly how 'harmless' pornography can be, imagine a ten-year-old boy named Juan. He likes to hang around the beach with his friends and he has heard them telling stories about the flabby old foreign man who often comes down to the beach and gives them money to rub suntan into his grey skin. They do not like him, but they have heard that he sometimes lets boys go to his house behind the high walls on the hill, where there is a television set, a swimming pool with clean water and plenty to eat and drink.

One day Juan strikes it 'lucky'. He is with his best friend when the man arrives, and there are few other boys around that day. The man is friendly, puts his arms around them and shows them more kindness than they have ever experienced. He buys them cold drinks from the vendor and asks them if they are hungry. When they say they are, he tells them it is lunchtime at his house and they are welcome to share a meal with him.

Everything in the big house is as Juan had imagined it: the sparkling pool, the table of food, the television set. The man lets them watch movies and pulls them to sit on his lap, where he tickles them and makes them laugh. Then he asks them if they would like to see a film he made with some of the other boys, and they open their eyes wide at the thought that their play-friends have made a movie.

This is no swashbuckling adventure film. There are no laughs and the boys seem to be having no fun. Juan cannot understand what they are doing. They have taken off all their clothes and the old man is with them in the film, touching them and putting their hands on his grey body. Juan feels uncomfortable and thinks he should go.

But the old man holds him back. There is no reason to feel uncomfortable, he says, just look at all your friends. They made the film, didn't they? They didn't feel uncomfortable. They were grateful for the food and the chance to come to the big house, and they came back again and again. Surely Juan doesn't believe that he is different from his friends? What would they think if they heard that? No, here's a good idea: why doesn't Juan 'star' in a film too, so that he can see that there is nothing unusual in what they are doing?

The old man holds Juan and his friend tighter, tugging at their grimy shorts until the boys are naked. They follow him, hesitant but convinced by the film of their friends and terrified of being seen as different, into a room where the man has put a small video camera in front of a dishevelled bed. They let him touch them – how can they say no when their friends obviously said yes? – and they follow his instructions to touch him, then put their mouths where he tells them.

And so Juan and his friend become film stars.

The images, though, stay in Juan's mind. Will anyone else see the film he made? What will they think? Will they think he wanted to do the things he did, or will they understand that it was not really his choice? Will they know he was unhappy about making the movie, or will they believe he enjoyed it?

Years later, long after the old man has moved on, Juan's 'fame' still haunts him. Now he is older, he knows that videos can be copied. He knows that you can hire them from video stores in the city. What if the man gave a copy of the film to someone else? Or if he sold it to one of the stores so that anyone who wanted to could watch it? He wonders whether people in other big houses, old men, young boys, friends, strangers, might be watching him as he lies naked, touching the old man.

Reports in the city newspapers say the police have arrested an illegal video copying ring and have confiscated hundreds of pornographic videos. What if 'his' film is among them and people in the city where he now lives get a chance to see it? Juan feels dirty, and guilty. Day in, day out, he is being exploited again and again.

And so pornography – moving pictures or still images – is used to entice children into sex, to lower their defences, to shame them into repeat performances, and to exploit them over and over. Long after the session in which the film was made or the photos taken, the thought of having participated in something 'unnatural' can haunt the children who were coerced into such activities.

For the exploiters, pornography is a tool they can use to titillate other young children, to share with like-minded friends and to ingratiate themselves with others seeking to exploit children sexually. It is also a way of making money and explains why unemployed men can live a relatively luxurious lifestyle which allows them the foreign travel and secure accommodation they need to continue their crimes.

That is why child pornography is not 'harmless'.

A circuit of some industrialised countries

Pornography is also a key that can open doors to finding and convicting exploiters of children, for not only do exploiters often use pornography to entrap children they are exploiting, they also use it for their self-aggrandisement. They 'star' in the videos or stills themselves, too, and so can be identified as exploiters by being recognised in pornographic recordings. Awareness of the link between child pornography and prostitution of children is absolutely vital.

Fred and Rosemary West, for example, who became infamous for the 'House of Horror' serial murders of young girls in England, are reported to have filmed themselves sexually exploiting their victims. Incredibly, they are said to have offered these video recordings to a local video rental store, where the link was not directly made between the activity captured on the video tapes and the fact that the young girls shown were being sexually abused and later murdered.

In many ways, although the Wests will go down in history as child murderers, the murders they committed were in fact probably not their main objective. They intended to have sex with children. They did have sex with children. They filmed themselves doing it. The murders were the ultimate turn-on, or were 'necessary' because they feared that people might find out what they were doing, and attempt to stop them, unless the children were silenced. It might be argued – without in any way diminishing the horror of the Wests' murderous actions – that murder was to the Wests little more than the inevitable outcome of their desire to sexually exploit young girls.

There is potentially much to be gained in the campaign to raise public awareness about the seriousness of child sexual exploitation, including the role of child pornography, by calling people like Fred and Rosemary West 'child sex exploiters' as well as 'murderers'.

The same is true of two other cases which shocked Europe in 1996.

Thomas Hamilton shattered the calm of the small town of Dunblane, Scotland, in March 1996 when he walked into the local primary school and opened fire on a class of six-year-olds, killing 16 of them and their teacher.

As always in cases like this, the first reaction to the senseless targeting of innocent children is disbelief. Next comes a desperate desire for understanding. 'Why?' parents demand. 'Why?' the newspapers scream out. 'Why?' right-thinking people who hear of the tragedy ask themselves. Rarely in such cases does anyone give an answer. In fact, there is no final answer to the question of why someone like Thomas Hamilton should eventually move from thought to deed, why on that fateful day his anger at the world, his frustration at his situation in it, turned from dark thoughts in his head to the guns in his hands and the decision to open fire.

But there are explanations for the weeks and months leading to that split second when the act was begun. And they show quite clearly that, although the guns in Hamilton's hands were the tools of death and destruction, it was his psychopathic desire to sexually exploit young children that led him to the school in Dunblane.

Thomas Hamilton was a paedophile. Although the word features in newspaper headlines every day now, it is generally misunderstood. Not everyone who has – or wants – sex with a child is a paedophile. Paedophilia is a quite specific term relating to people whose psychiatric profile identifies them as someone who has an urge to sexually abuse prepubescent children.

This profile contains a whole list of characteristics which can be observed and, importantly, documented and acted upon. First of all, paedophiles tend to manoeuvre themselves into situations where they have easy access to children. Many of them become teachers, social workers, priests. They might organise clubs for children, where they can observe the children, gain their trust and become close to them. And they create opportunities to isolate themselves and the children, so that they can wield power over them in a context where parents cannot intervene. Thomas Hamilton ran sports clubs for young boys. He seems to have built his life around these clubs, working with passion to find venues for his meetings. He ingratiated himself with the boys who became members and made sure they were a little scared of him, although not too much to drive them away.

Hamilton took 'his boys' on camping trips where they were entirely in his control. He made them take off their shirts 'to make them tough' and took photos of them in camp, as well as in the showers at the club.

In this, Hamilton offered another glaring example of the classic paedophile profile: paedophiles are known to collect visual images of children. The photos not only have an element of voyeurism associated with child pornography, they 'fix' the age of the child, so that the paedophile can relive his prepubescent fantasies even when the child has grown up and moved on.

When parents started complaining that their sons told them Hamilton was domineering, abusive and liked to touch and photograph them, his access to the rooms he used for his club was denied. He appealed, wrote furious letters to the authorities and, in an episode whose significance lies heavy on those who recognise paedophile behaviour, sought an interview with the headmistress of the school where the club meetings were held.

Her reports of that meeting illustrate another characteristic of the paedophile profile. Hamilton was, she said, 'uncomfortable' in her presence. He would not shake her hand and seemed 'ill at ease with himself'. It is known that male paedophiles are often uneasy with adult company, particularly adult women.

This list of indicative traits, when enumerated together, add up overwhelmingly to 'classic' paedophile behaviour. Yet throughout the months, even years, leading up to the murder of the Dunblane children, no-one labelled Hamilton a paedophile. 'He acted strange,' people said. 'He looked a normal kind of person but we didn't like him. He kept himself to himself and he seemed a bit weird to us.'

There seems to have been almost total lack of coordination and communication among the various actors in the story who might have intervened: despite parents' complaints, investigating authorities put Hamilton's behaviour down as 'inappropriate' but stopped short of classifying it as potentially paedophile. Different local authority departments in the same town, and equivalent departments in different towns, did not communicate with each other or share information, presumably because Hamilton was seen as 'odd' but was not labelled as a paedophile and because, in any case, there were no regulations covering recording or sharing information on suspected or even recognised paedophile behaviour in the United Kingdom.

Hamilton was consequently never thoroughly investigated nor offered therapy or treatment. His enormous collection of photos of boys in states of semi-nakedness was labelled as 'unhealthy' but not questioned.

Instead, various authorities put artificial hurdles in his path, in the hope that the problem might somehow just go away. He was denied use of room space for his meetings. He was cut out of groups which might have helped him to organise his clubs and camping trips. His access to 'his boys' – the entire focus of his life – was gradually shut off.

But he was given a firearms licence and allowed to buy guns.

He wrote to the Queen of England asking her to intervene so that he could continue his chosen lifestyle. He was running out of options.

What it was that made him realise, on that March morning in 1996, that there were no options left, we may never know. But the action he took will remain part of our history, and will go down in the annals of sexual exploitation of children as a paedophile act that has still hardly been recognised as such. Even in the aftermath of this tragedy, those who are desperate to reach out and do something to stop it happening again are concentrating almost entirely on the need to control firearms. In reality, more emphasis must be placed on the need to identify paedophile behaviour through coordinated reporting of isolated incidents and to intervene speedily to investigate suspected paedophile cases. Although paedophilia cannot be 'cured', behaviour can be controlled and certainly community action can be taken to limit access to opportunities for exploitation or to such things as firearms licences.

In what has come to be known as 'the Dutroux case' in Belgium in August 1996, however, there seem to have been fewer options for preventative action.

On 15 August 1996, police in Marcinelles, a suburb of Charleroi, Belgium, rescued two young girls – Laetitia Delhez, 14, and Sabine Dardenne, 12 – from sexual captivity. Laetitia had disappeared on 9 August between the local swimming pool and her home in Bertrix, in the south-east of Belgium, and Sabine had been missing since 29 May when she did not arrive at school in Kain, a suburb of Tournai in the south-west of the country. The rescue followed police requests for a media 'blackout' on the question of the missing girls and on speculation concerning two teenagers, Eefje Lambreks (19) and An Marchal (17), both from Limbourg in eastern Belgium, and two eight-year-olds, Julie Lejeune and Mélissa Russo, missing since 24 June 1995 from near their homes in Grace-Hollogne, near Liège.

Laetitia and Sabine reported that they had been literally plucked off the streets, drugged and held in a dungeon measuring 4.6 metres by 3.6 metres. Police took into custody Marc Dutroux, 39, an unemployed builder, who had served time in prison for sexual offences including, at the end of 1993, a conviction for building cells to hold children captive.

It transpired that the two girls had not been the first occupants of the dungeon in the basement of Dutroux's house.

Under questioning, Dutroux offered to lead police to the graves of Julie and Mélissa, who had been held in the same dungeon. While Dutroux was serving a short prison term in early 1996, he said, they had been allowed to starve to death by his second wife, Michelle Martin, and Bernard Weinstein, the man who had abducted them in the first place. Dutroux claimed that he had given Weinstein and a lodger, Michel Lelievre, approximately £1200 to feed the girls and look after them and that, when he had returned and found one of them dead and the other dying, he had killed Weinstein and buried all three bodies.

Lelievre and Martin were subsequently charged by Belgian police on counts of imprisoning children. A business associate, Jean-Michel Nihoul, was also charged with criminal association. Before the grisly details of this story were out, however, the bodies of Eefje and An had also been found.

It seems that all the girls had fallen into the hands of a highly organised paedophile ring. Dutroux, despite being 'unemployed', owned a number of substantial properties. A number of 'supergrasses' had told police that Dutroux had offered them money to kidnap young girls and that he was building dungeons in the cellar of one of his houses. He was known by the police to have links to international networks through which stolen cars and drugs were trafficked and which would provide means to traffic human merchandise too.

Experience of such crimes certainly suggests that all the elements were in place. The girls were abducted unwillingly and certainly drugs were used to keep them subservient. They were imprisoned and sexually abused. Business connections seem to have been in place so that the girls might be trafficked among members of the ring and, presumably, further afield. Multiple properties suggests that the girls would be kept moving, so that their tracks would be covered. Money would change hands as the girls' bodies were sold for sex.

This ring of sex would operate in much the same way that drug circuits do, or stolen car networks. The 'product' would be obtained, sold to customers and on-sold as necessary, to keep it moving and out of sight, and huge profits would result. In the case of paedophile networks, however, the 'product' is a child and the purpose of the trade is child sex.

In the months following the discovery of the young girls in Dutroux's house, more and more questions were raised in Belgium about the nature of paedophile rings such as those Dutroux reportedly serviced, and the protection of paedophile activity by influential personalities. A commission of enquiry heard how rivalry among different sectors of the police in Belgium, particularly along Flemish–French lines of demarcation, led to investigations being hampered, interrupted and even ignored – police had searched the house where Dutroux held the girls three times without finding Julie and Mélissa, who were imprisoned just metres away. And the Commission concluded, 'based on the relevant evidence, that Nihoul, Dutroux, Derochette and their accomplices may have been protected'. Far-reaching changes were announced in the wake of the Commission's report: the three-tier police system in Belgium would be moulded into one federal force; a number of high-ranking law enforcement figures were suspended and Belgian Prime Minister Jean-Luc Dehaene promised a thorough review of laws.

Despite the evidence that the girls imprisoned by Marc Dutroux and his accomplices could have been found earlier and might therefore have survived, however, it is difficult to see what could have been done to stop them being taken in the first place. They were loved children from good homes. They were not in any sense of the word immediately identifiable as 'vulnerable', as so many children in the world today are vulnerable to sexual slavery. They were abducted from the streets of a relatively 'safe' country not normally seen as a hotbed of the child sex trade.

Undoubtedly there are questions to be asked about the role of law enforcement, given Dutroux's known criminal behaviour, about the severity of punishment, amidst reports that he served only three years of a 13-year conviction for rape and abduction of teenage girls, and about bungling and unacceptable interference in the case once it was under way, but it is almost impossible to see what more could have been done to stop the abductions happening in the first place.

This is one of the most frightening aspects of the kinds of sexual exploitation of children that take place in so-called 'industrialised' societies. Often so many of the elements of vulnerability common to the children of Asia and South America – such as poverty and low status of the girl child, for example – are absent. Instead, the key to preventing children from being exploited seems to lie in the profile of the exploiter. What was known about Dutroux was the key not only to finding the children who died but also to protecting them in the first place.

In an attempt to focus attention on the client/intermediary in child sex cases, many industrialised countries have begun serious review of the nature of staff employed in their social services. In Australia and in the United Kingdom, cases have come to light of exploiters infiltrating social service networks in order to have easy access to children. In these instances, the children may be vulnerable as a result of family breakdown or sexual abuse at home.

In early 1996, Bob Carr, Premier of the Australian state of New South Wales, ordered an immediate investigation into allegations that Australian paedophiles had used the New South Wales child welfare system to obtain children for sexual exploitation. The allegations had been made during hearings at a Commission of Enquiry into abuses in the New South Wales Police Service, an enquiry headed by Justice James Wood.

The Wood Commission heard the gruesome story of two 'rent boys', Andrew Tregurtha and Terry Hitchins, who had run away from home and, at the age of 13, had begun to sell sex on the streets of the infamous King's Cross area of Sydney to survive.

The two boys were taken into care at a place called The Refuge, in Liverpool Street, King's Cross. It was a shelter run by the Homeless Children's Association in the late 1970s and early 1980s and boasted a number of eminent Australians among its patrons, including former Australian Prime Minister Bob Hawke.[23] Through The Refuge, the boys were introduced into paedophile rings by the men who were running the centre, and were 'expected to be part of the scene'.[24] According to reports, all the children who stayed there were. But Tregurtha and Hitchins could only take so much. Eventually, used and then discarded as they reached 16 and became 'too old' for paedophile preferences, they took what was to be a horrific way out of their sexual slavery.

In 1981, Tregurtha murdered paedophiles Peter Parkes and Constantine Giannaris, at the time Greek Consul in Sydney. That same year, Hitchins and two friends, Stephen Elliot and Eric de Vries, murdered Raymond Savage, a Sydney taxi driver. Later that year, Hitchins and another friend, Zolan Nemec, murdered taxi driver John Collins.

Tregurtha and de Vries committed suicide in custody. Hitchins, Elliott and Nemec were jailed.

But the tragic story of these young boys abused first by a society that saw them condemned to life on the streets and then exploited by paedophile networks which had thoroughly infiltrated the very system set up to care for them, opened up a can of worms relating to Australia's social services and the potential they offer for sexual exploitation of children.

A senior state government welfare officer, identified only as 'T7' before the Wood Commission, made money over a number of years by selling homosexual child pornography by mail. In 1994, he was charged with hiding 6000 obscene photographs in a bank deposit box under a false name. He reportedly had a stock of 30 000 negatives of under-age boys in explicit poses. Incredibly, he took the negatives to shop-front photographic developing outlets to have the pictures made up for his customers, but was never reported.

When the Commission asked T7 why he sold obscene photographs, he replied, 'Without appearing vain, I wanted some acknowledgement or recognition of my sort of artistry.'

T7 is not an artist. He is an exploiter of children and makes money by selling their souls. His pornographic 'creations' are no more than a record of this despicable trade. At the same time, for 27 years, he was an officer in the child welfare services and, as such, had access to the personal files of 'children at risk' and children who had been made wards of state. It must never be forgotten that such children are already suffering. They are frequently from broken homes, where they may already have been sexually abused. They sometimes have lost one or both parents. They may have been already exposed to drugs, ill health, dysfunctioning relationships. Society steps in and offers them something new: in theory, a caring environment, a secure place where they can feel safe, the promise of a new beginning and the chance to rebuild a life that has been torn apart.

Then T7 picks up the child's file and makes a note of the details. He told the Wood Commission of how he would read the files 'from cover to cover', steal the photographs from them and take them home. Then he would call on the children and invite them to visit him at home.

An unemployed boy identified in the Commission as 'V1' was invited to T7's apartment and was given £30 to 'hit him with a belt, masturbate him and pose naked for photographs'. Although the file had shown that V1 had already complained about suicidal feelings, T7 denied that he might in any way be considered 'fragile'.

Added to the fragility of unemployment, homelessness, drug dependency, ill health and a host of other vulnerabilities that too many young people face in today's industrialised societies, the evidence shows quite clearly that, in many instances, the very systems set up to receive and reassure them harbour people who are waiting to pounce and sexually exploit them. As a youth worker in Sydney told *The Bulletin* magazine in April 1996 about the boys of King's Cross who became murderers, 'The boys became totally desensitised. They felt they had no value as human beings and therefore no one else had any value. Most of the boys involved in that lifestyle ended up completely fucked.'

In August 1996, the Christian Brothers of Australia were ordered to pay £1.5 million to 260 former students who had been sexually abused while in their care in the 1930s. While expressing outrage at the crimes that had been committed, the Brothers' spokesperson claimed that the actions had been of individuals, not the organisation itself. However, organisations are made up of individuals and responsibility for the actions of individuals who profess a particular organisation's 'membership' is necessarily collective. The Australian Government seems belatedly to have realised this and now leads the way in bringing both individuals and organisations to task for reported cases of sexual exploitation of children today and in the documented past.

As a result, the newly elected government of Prime Minister John Howard in mid-1996 set up an 'Inquiry into Allegations of Paedophile Activities', headed by a public servant, Mr Chris Hunt. Announcing the enquiry on a trip to Bangkok, Minister for Foreign Affairs Alexander Downer promised that the enquiry would 'reveal the truth' about alleged paedophile activities by officers of the Australian Government Department of Foreign Affairs and Trade, and its overseas development agencies, AusAID and Austrade. 'The enquiry will not only concern itself with the behaviours of individual officers,' Mr Downer said, 'but will also examine the systems, structure and culture of portfolio agencies to see if they have been adequate in the effective management of Australia's representatives and their behaviour while overseas.' Effectively, the Australian Government had decided to take a good look at itself and at the sexual exploitation of children by its own members.

Among its terms of reference is looking at whether any reports of sexual exploitation of children by overseas-based Australian Government employees have been 'hushed up'. This is a serious issue, because it seems that very often allegations of exploitation have gone unreported, or have not been investigated, for fear of 'diplomatic incidents' and because diplomats, in particular, have influential friends.

The list of reports received by the Hunt Enquiry in the earliest days of its work reads like a script for a horror/detective thriller: according to reports, Australian aid money has in the past been used by diplomats stationed overseas to establish schools and orphanages, so that exploiters could have easier access to vulnerable children; Australian intelligence services intercepted child pornography being exchanged between diplomats in diplomatic mail bags, but did not report the incident for more than a decade; diplomats under investigation for sexual exploitation of children, or specifically known to have exploited children sexually, as in the case of an Australian diplomat based in an unnamed Asian country who impregnated an under-age Muslim girl, were routinely transferred to other postings where they could continue their activities.

'Having sex with children is as Australian as going to the beach,' Steve Biddulf, an Australian child psychologist and writer, is quoted as saying.[25] But it is of course ridiculous to point the finger at Australia and not recognise that the sexual exploitation of children, whether commercial or for personal gratification only, by diplomats and government servants stationed overseas occurs regardless of the country of origin. It is not nationality that makes a sex exploiter but the criminal urge to abuse children. An unnamed politician from central Sweden, on assignment in Asia, was reported in the Swedish daily *Aftonbladet* as having married a 14-year-old Thai girl, who had borne him a child. Difficult as this might be to accept, what is even more horrific is the fact that the Thai child was his fifth wife. Over ten years, this representative of a so-called 'civilised' country had married and discarded four more child-brides from Poland, Russia, Brazil and Thailand. The man abused the children sexually and was violent, causing one of the girls to lose an eye. Immigration officials reportedly 'shut their eyes'[26] as long as the marriage did not last more than two years.

What has singled out the Australian Government in this issue is the brave steps it has taken to do something about alleged corruption within. There is perhaps no better example of this than the case of John Scott Holloway, one of Australia's most senior diplomats, a former ambassador to Cambodia and, according to those who worked with him for many years in postings overseas, 'a really nice man'.

On 30 April 1996, Holloway came before Magistrate Michael Somes charged with having sex with a child under 16 between 14 July and 30 September 1994 in Phnom Penh, Cambodia. Holloway, 53, denied allegations that he engaged in sexual activity with young boys while serving in his official posts, arguing that his open homosexuality had simply made him a target for 'gay bashers'. In November 1996, charges against Holloway were dropped when a trial judge ordered that there were discrepancies in statements made by the young Cambodian boy – no surprise to those who have attempted to follow through legal action in cases of alleged sexual exploitation of children. Such observers caution that exploited children are often confused, contradictory and emotionally torn between attachments they have formed with their exploiters and the shame they feel. Hubert Van Gijseghem, professor of psychology at the University of Montreal, Canada, says that 'false allegations from children are very rare; the figure is estimated in studies at between one and three per cent'. Van Gijseghem also suggests that, while accusations made spontaneously are almost always true, problems set in when a 'well-intentioned adult puts suggestive questions with a precise idea in mind'. The possibility of obtaining clear statements from the child becomes even more unlikely, he says, when the child is forced to undergo questioning several times. 'His reaction is to say to himself that no-one believes him, because they keep asking him the same questions. And so he ends up taking back what he said, just to get some peace.' Van Gijseghem concludes that there must be 'uncontaminated' and 'non-contaminating' questioning and that professional investigators must learn to handle interrogation of potentially abused children in such a way that their evidence is reliable. Above all, he says, the first version of the story that children give is undoubtedly the most reliable and should be recorded.[27]

Despite the inconclusive nature of the Holloway case, and the fact that the way the child witness was handled failed to bring justice to either the potentially abused child or the potentially falsely accused Holloway, it is nevertheless significant that the Australian Government proceeded with investigation of a senior diplomat, and that it did so publicly.

Holloway was charged under Australia's Crimes (Child Sex Tourism) Amendment Act of 1994, an act of extraterritoriality which allows Australian courts to try Australian citizens and residents for child sex crimes committed in other countries, even if such acts are not a crime in that country. Under Division 2/50BA, 'a person must not, while outside Australia, engage in sexual intercourse with a person who is under 16'. The penalty: imprisonment for 17 years. Holloway was the second Australian to have been investigated under the 1994 Act; earlier in 1996 another Australian, Anthony Carr, was jailed for two years for having sex with a six-year-old girl in Manila, Philippines.

But before we go travelling again, let us stay on the streets of the world's industrialised countries, ironically in this instance often called 'developed' countries. For there is no doubt that children are sexually exploited and sold for sex not only when they are at the mercy of social services, caretakers and others who have responsibility for their welfare, but whenever economic and social circumstances force upon them weaknesses of which unscrupulous exploiters can take advantage.

Reports of children being exploited while in residential homes in Clywd, Wales, and in Cheshire, England, shocked the people of Great Britain in June 1996, but there has been no such emotional reaction to repeated reports of children as young as 12 and 13 selling sex on the streets of some of Britain's major cities.

Dawn Shields began her life on the streets of Bradford, northern England, at the age of 15. It had ended there by the time she was 19. Articles about her in the British press in February 1996[28] tell a story that is familiar to those who work with children who have been prostituted.

Dawn was one of many young girls between the ages of 12 and 16 who walk the streets of England. Estimates in 1996 put at between 3000 and 5000 the number of children in the sex trade in Britain. Many of these children enter the 'profession' when they become addicted to drugs like crack cocaine and need to pay for their habit. Men – pimps – looking to earn a little extra money from their drug dealing keep the children in drugs and make tidy profits from selling their wasted bodies to anyone who fancies them. They can earn £120 a night even in areas where unemployment and economic hardship make such sums difficult to come by.

Dawn's case is typical. Her father died when she was eight and she seemed always to be looking for a replacement strong man in her life. She was a 'problem child' for school teachers who complained that she dressed 'like a hooker'. But she was not looking for clients, she was looking for 'my own flat, money and a baby that loves me – that's what I want'. Dawn was looking for the family life that had disappeared with her father.

She found a man who gave her the baby she wanted but did not want to marry her. He slapped her and screamed abuse at her and put her to work to earn money for his drug habit. Seven nights a week, out on streets where, according to adult prostitutes, 'the punters are looking for the younger girls because they're cheaper'.

Dawn's 'man' was into cocaine and had gambling debts and she had to go home each night with at least £120 for him or she would be beaten. She took customers until she had enough money to go home to the 'family life' she had wanted so much. Officers of the local social services tried to help Dawn, but she never felt she needed them. Men show their love by beating women, she believed, 'they beat you because they love you so much they are afraid you would go with somebody else'.

Dawn was taken to hospital on several occasions with broken ribs, back injuries and strangle marks on her neck. She never pressed charges. When a friend tried to intervene to stop Dawn's pimp beating her, the pimp raped her. 'He thought he was God,' she reported. 'Dawn was unconscious and he was raping me.

'She begged and begged me to drop charges against him, saying she still loved him. By the end she was like a shell of what she was. She stayed with him because she saw no way of leaving him.

'One time my doorbell went at five in the morning. She was standing there on one leg. He had attacked her with a baseball bat, her knee was all over the place ... The violence became worse and then she began eating drugs and became addicted.'

And the police? 'The vice squad would see her on the street with a black eye,' Dawn's friend relates, 'and say "So Dawn, walk into another lamp-post?" and laugh.'

At first Dawn would file a report with the police, only to see the pimp receive bail so that he could come back and beat her again for reporting him. What was the point? The only escape would have been to run away, but Dawn knew he would never let her go; she was his meal ticket.

Dawn had no money of her own to pay for the drugs she got from other dealers. In the end she was murdered because she could not pay her debts. She was driven to a quiet mountain road and strangled. The Criminal Compensations Board turned down a request for funds from Dawn's mother, who is now raising Dawn's baby, on the grounds that 'the deceased's criminal convictions make an award inappropriate'.

The newspaper article sums up very well society's attitude to a drug-addicted child who sells herself on the streets: 'Place of death unknown. Cause of death unknown. Just another dead tart.'

The British Home Office still claims that the child sex trade in Great Britain 'is not a widespread problem' because in 1990 only 30 boys and three girls were charged with soliciting. Yet it is quite obvious that most police officers simply caution the children they see on the street corners, unwilling to take them into custody because they know it will not help and that the children might face retribution from their pimps if they do not bring home the money. Their only recourse is to charitable and youth groups who work with children on the streets in full awareness of the limitations they face. Street-wise Youth, for example, works with boys in the sex trade in London, some as young as 14. Tony Whitehead, Streetwise director, believes it is wrong to consider the children as 'prostitutes'. 'These are just kids on the street in a mess,' he says. 'Prostitution is a means of survival for them, as others may turn to begging or crime or drug-dealing.'

Whitehead confirms that many of the children – at least 60 per cent – come from homes in which they have been sexually abused. 'If they are going to be abused,' he says, 'they feel they may as well be paid for it and escape from their abuser at home or in care.'

This story is repeated throughout the cities of Western Europe.

Amongst the elegant architecture of Seville, Spain, clients seek out children for sex. Scandals surrounding well-known nightclubs which were little more than fronts for child sex rings reverberated through Spain, not so much because the children found there were as young as 14, but because the client list included a number of prominent society figures.[29]

In Palermo, Italy, a police raid on a squalid inner city district on 30 June 1996 uncovered a child pornography business and a crowd of young children, *picciriddi* in Italian, kept in virtual slavery. The oldest child was 14; the youngest five.

In 1989, a book published by one of France's best-known publishing houses detailed just one aspect of the child sex trade operating in Paris. It describes one of the city's great parks where at night car headlights pick up the spectre-like figures of young children in the shadows, waiting for customers. One of the children was named Alexis. He wrote the book and gave it a romantic-sounding title that belies the horrors he relates: *The boy from the Bois de Boulogne.*[30]

In the great cities of Europe, on the streets of the New World's capitals, in care homes provided by 'civilised' societies, children are being sold for sex. Pimps and drug dealers are making money from them to fuel their greed and criminal habits. Men from all walks of life are buying them. Not only paedophiles but, according to Alexis, 'fathers of families'.

And we have not finished with Europe yet, for there is a growing phenomenon in the child sex trade that has resulted from the end of the Cold War, the breaking down of frontiers between West and Eastern Europe, the closing of options for exploiters who once travelled to Asia and South America to indulge their vile habits, and the pulls of consumer society so long held in check by the straitjacket of communism.

Alina shares a concrete pipe with rats and cockroaches in the underground labyrinth beneath the park in front of the Gara du Nord, the main railway station in Bucharest, Romania. She is 16 years old and was expelled from an orphanage because of unruly behaviour. She fled to join her brother at the Gara du Nord but met, instead, a pimp named Suraj.[31] He recruits young children to his 'team' by raping them, ensuring that their view of their sexuality is debased and their defences are down.

Alina has two walls of protection against the abuse Suraj dishes out. She has a friend, Valentin, who started selling sex in the railway station when he was 14 and who knows how to survive. Valentin looks after the younger children as well as he can and is their only link to anything like the parental affection and guidance children should have as their right.

And Alina has her bag of glue, which she takes a deep breath from and then knots and hides away in her pocket.

Alina is one of hundreds of children who shelter in the pipes around the Gara du Nord, most of whom are forced to sell themselves to survive. Thousands more hang around the parks and on street corners throughout Romania. According to Romanian Save the Children, there are between 5000 and 6000 children in Bucharest who live on the streets.[32] They are the abandoned children of post-communist Romania, left behind in the scramble for democracy, capitalist consumer goods and a lifestyle that puts money and self before duty and children.

In the 1960s Romanian dictator Nicolae Ceausescu stridently promoted population growth, banning contraception and abortions for any woman with fewer than four children. His moves to increase the masses led to untold poverty, unwanted children and more people than the infrastructure could possibly handle. After his overthrow and execution, it was a matter of survival of the fittest. Part of his legacy was a country with more than half the total number of cases of paediatric AIDS in Europe, ensuring that Romania's orphanages would be filled to capacity with children with AIDS, abandoned by their families.

AIDS threatens the children who work the streets, too, as do Hepatitis B, malnutrition, tuberculosis and syphilis. Social workers say that 95 per cent of the children trapped in the sex trade have some sexually transmitted disease. Their fate is unthinkable. Despite the dismantling of communist ideologies, the bureaucracy and mindset of former communist ministries remain. The wheels of change turn very slowly and the children get left behind by social services overwhelmed with the heavy load they have to bear and bogged down in the machinery of getting things done. Many, many of the children will be dead before a way to improve their lot is found.

In the meantime, they are prey to pimps and exploiters who, oblivious to their fragility, poor health and the real likelihood of disease transmission, sell them at £1.00 or £2.00 a time to local customers and visiting paedophiles.

Day by day the trains go in and out of the station, hinting at a world beyond the concrete pipes of Alina's underground hell. But it is a world that Alina no longer thinks about. The only world she can escape to is the one conjured up in the noxious fumes of her glue bag.

Some Romanian children, however, have boarded the trains and planes that take them away from Romania. In the confusion which followed the downfall of Ceausescu, 10 000 Romanian children were adopted overseas. Once the initial rush was over, mechanisms were put in place to approve applications by foreign couples to adopt Romanian orphans. In those first months, however, there was no supervision and many children disappeared without trace. Today there are still few regulations governing children taken overseas on 'temporary foster' visits, or to summer camps in the west.

It is well known that many children have been introduced in this way into West European paedophile and pornography rings. The British police advised researchers Helena Karlen and Christina Hagner that they know of several British men sentenced for sexual offences against children who regularly visit Romania and other Eastern European countries, although the nature of their interest in these countries has not yet been confirmed. Many of these men work under the guise of 'charitable organisations'.

Bernard Lynn founded an organisation he called 'Friends in Romania' in the early 1990s. He and friend Graham Sampson visited a small town in the Romanian countryside and introduced themselves as charity workers. They were well received and as a result of their abundant generosity were soon entrusted with the children of the town. They filled their rented apartment with computer games and toys the children could only dream of. They had to return to England but promised to return soon to 'their children'.

On their return, Lynn and Sampson were apprehended by the British police for sexual abuse of two English boys and were sentenced to 10 and 13 years in jail respectively. Lynn still writes to 'his children' from prison, promising to return soon. The children think he is in hospital. When he is finally released, there is as yet nothing stopping him returning to Romania. Although he has confessed to British police that he abused young boys while in Romania, the British police have not been able to interest their Romanian counterparts in the case.

Indeed, the Romanian National Prosecution Authority insists that sexual abuse of children is 'unusual' in their country. It is true that during the communist era sexual exploitation of children was entirely unknown – because no one was allowed to suggest that it existed. There are still no official data for sexual exploitation in Romania.

The whole issue is exacerbated by the fact that Romania still fixes the age of sexual consent at 14. As a result, exploiters of Romanian children feel that they are protected by the law in many instances, and argue that the child 'consented' to sex in the railway station, orphanage, rented room, bushes in the park or wherever. For the children faced with no home, no income, no social support, no future and the fear of retribution if they speak out, it must be comparatively easy to 'consent'.

In recent years, too, the exploited children of Romania have been found in other parts of the world. In 1994 a young Romanian girl was found murdered in a Turkish brothel. Romanian minors have been reported in Cyprus, Greece, Italy and Holland. Indeed, Romanian boys dominate the trafficking of boys for sex in Europe. Boys between the ages of ten and 14 turn up in Berlin and Amsterdam, often in groups 'supervised' by an adult. Estimates in early 1996 suggest that as many as 1000 Romanian boys sell sex on the streets of Berlin, and 200 in Amsterdam. Local boys complain that the 'cheap imports' bring down the prices.

Trafficking of children for sexual slavery from Eastern Europe to the west is not confined to Romania. Swedish police have reported that hundreds of boys from a number of Baltic countries have been trafficked into Sweden in recent years. They are 'adopted' from orphanages in Poland and elsewhere and end up in pornography production houses and nightclubs. The Swedish arm of the international law enforcement agency, Interpol, confirms that Polish orphans have also been sold to Holland and Canada, and that Swedish paedophiles are reported to have visited Polish orphanages to abuse the children there and then arrange their travel to the west.

Karlen and Hagner have traced trafficking routes that make the map of Europe look like a bowl of spaghetti.

A 16-year-old Lithuanian girl was found in an Israeli brothel. Girls are trafficked from Estonia, Latvia and Lithuania to Poland, Germany, Holland and elsewhere. Children arrive from Belarus, Russia and the Ukraine to the Baltic States and then are often trafficked again to the west and south, to countries like Spain and Portugal.

There are even reports of 'travelling brothels' along the borders dividing East from West in Europe. Trucks reportedly travel along the borders with young children in the back, as a 'service' to frequent travellers.

In Hungary, this translates as 'road prostitution'. On the M1 motorway between Vienna and Budapest, and then along the E75 towards Romania, lorry drivers have found a whole new meaning for the phrase 'truck stop'. In lay-bys along the road, they take young children into their cabs for sex. Foreign tourists, especially Germans, have access to the same 'roadside services'. Most of the children come from poor country areas of Hungary, but there are also many from other countries of Eastern Europe.

Most of the children are recruited through advertisements offering work in clubs as dancers or barmaids, or in homes as au-pairs or domestic servants. The recruiter undertakes to take care of all the paperwork and provides the girls with false documents, putting them in an illegal situation which increases their vulnerability and makes them, in the eyes of the law, criminals with no recourse to justice. The girls sign promissory notes to cover these 'set-up' costs and are thus trapped in a form of debt bondage that means they cannot just walk away even when they realise that they have been deceived.

After this first recruitment into the sex trade, girls and boys may be traded several times so that, like the children trafficked through Asia, they disappear and their tracks are covered.

In places like Berlin, the trafficked children from Eastern Europe are gradually replacing Asian children, since it is easier and cheaper to bring a child across a land border than by air or across greater distances. Most of the girls who arrive in the west are kept in bars or brothels.

The boys, on the other hand, meet customers in the streets or at railway stations. The central railway station in Berlin is a good example. Soon after the fall of the Berlin Wall in 1989, the station was crowded with boys from East Germany, joined soon after by children from Poland and Romania. There are an estimated 2000 boys involved in the sex trade in Berlin alone, looking for a way to survive in a city they were told would offer them an escape from the poverty of the east. Boys as young as nine years of age have been found working in the station, although most of the younger children seem to be 'adopted' by German paedophiles and taken to the 'comfort' of a private apartment. They reappear some years later when they have outgrown the paedophile's fantasies.

Paedophile rings, coercion and trafficking, street-based prostitution and drug addiction, abuse in the home and in care, disease and death. The so-called 'developed' countries of Europe offer a comprehensive case study in the variety that commercial sexual exploitation of children can take. But there's more.

In recent years, there have been reports of a new twist to the tale. Although reports of sham marriages and adoptions from Eastern Europe into West European countries like Germany are undocumented, a number of organisations working with exploited children in Europe insist that they take place. A group of Polish journalists also claims to have infiltrated a network centring on Poland and Germany which arranges sham marriages between Polish women and German men. The women arrive in Germany with 'children from a previous relationship' in tow and, presumably, go through legal marriages with German men. Some time later, however, the women return to Poland, never to be heard of again. The children do not. They remain with their new 'step-fathers' who introduce them into paedophile networks where they find whole new 'families' of adult men to 'take care' of them.

These reports have yet to be investigated but, in a world where eight-year-old girls can be plucked from the calm of a suburban Belgian street to die in a dungeon where they have been enslaved as sexual toys, anything seems possible.

2 It happens here too: More about the global market in child sex

The United States Government thinks it has an answer to the question of what more could have been done in the Belgian Dutroux case. On 25 June 1996, before the discovery of the Charleroi dungeon, the White House put out a statement in the form of a memorandum to the Attorney General of the United States, Janet Reno. It called on her to 'develop a plan for the implementation of a national sexual predator and child molester registration system'. The memo, signed 'William J. Clinton', called upon the Attorney General's Department to 'work with all 50 States, the Congress, the Judiciary, and all appropriate Federal agencies on a plan for such a system so that law enforcement officers at every level will have access to information on all sexual offenders in the United States and share this information with one another'.

Cynical musings about the timing of this action coinciding with the final stages of the run-up to the 1996 Presidential election aside, the concept of a national 'tracking system' for known sexual exploiters of children in the United States has a longer history.

On the North American trail

In 1994, the Violent Crime Control and Law Enforcement Act (Crime Bill) included a section known as the Jacob Wetterling Crimes Against Children and Sexually Violent Offender Registration Act. The Wetterling Act, as it is known, encouraged states to register child molesters and other sexually violent offenders.

Registration, however, has no impact at all if the information collected is not looked upon as a tool of preventive action. It was not until mid-1996 that President Clinton built upon the Wetterling Act's potential by signing what came to be known as 'Megan's Law', in memory of seven-year-old Megan Kanka, whose sexual abuse and murder at the hands of a man who had served three jail sentences for sexual abuse, prompted public outrage and subsequent review of the law against sexual abuse of children. Megan's Law made community notification of registered sex offenders mandatory. It requires states to make public relevant information about child molesters and sexually violent offenders who are released from prison or placed on parole. Under Megan's Law, it is argued, Marc Dutroux's early release from prison in Belgium after a child rape conviction would have been known to the people of Charleroi and his predatory presence on their streets would have been signalled.

The memo to Attorney General Janet Reno calling for development of a national registration system was an obvious next step in the drive to keep track of sex offenders. Plugged into a national database network, state registers would effectively become elements of a national register, so that sex offenders could also be tracked across state lines.

'Together we can make the image in the mirror of society one that reflects the innocence and joy of childhood,' Assistant Attorney General Laurie Robinson told delegates at the Stockholm Congress in August 1996.[1] Not surprisingly, however, many people believe that what will be reflected in the US mirror is a parade of witches.

'Witch-hunt', some civil rights groups have called the registration system. 'Spooked by abuse', the newspaper headlines say. And, indeed, there is a real fear, that in the face of the horrendous crimes against children committed by those who sexually exploit them, society will overreact. Lock the children up for safety. Do not let them walk down the street alone. Keep the sexes separated. Trust no one. Tighten the rules. Presume the worst. Lock up all the gays. Outlaw prostitution. Ban sex.

There has to be some calm and moderation. Reports in September and October 1996 of a six-year-old American boy suspended from school on sexual harassment charges when he kissed a girl friend show only too clearly that adults can simply go too far in their desire to protect children. Lines have to be drawn somewhere, but the difficulty is knowing exactly where.

Debate of a proposed new city ordinance in San Mateo, California, which would require all those who work with children to submit to fingerprinting and checks for criminal records before they can be employed, even as volunteers, divided the community clearly down the middle.

Some were wholeheartedly in favour of the move. 'I think everybody should be fingerprinted,' Claire Mack, a San Mateo City Council member, is quoted as saying.[2] 'I say shut every damn door you can so no child in society gets hurt.'

'It would be an absolute nightmare,' Marc Nelson, president of the San Mateo American Little League, complained. 'I can guarantee you that this would come back and eat us alive.'

Detractors point to the fact that fewer than 10 per cent of the 100 000 reported instances of child sexual abuse each year in the United States occur in institutional settings such as clubs, schools or sports groups. By far the majority of incidents of abuse which are reported occur in the home or in the local neighbourhood. More than half the rapes reported in the United States are committed against young girls below the age of 18. Sixteen per cent of these rapes involve girls younger than 12. And the younger the victim, the more likely it is that the rapist is a member of the family or a family friend – there is a one-in-five chance that the rapist is the girl's father. The bottom line, it seems, is that it is vitally important to do the homework, know the facts and attack the problem on a logical, researched basis.

Whereas the national registration system seems to do this – targeting those who have already been convicted of sex offences and more than three-quarters of whom scientific research shows are likely to offend again within two years – the fingerprinting and check system looks to be ill-thought-out and to be missing the target.

Even when the action undertaken seems to be appropriate, though, public *reaction* is less predictable and, by mid-1997, as governments in many countries began to crack down on sex offenders, questions were justifiably being asked about how witch-hunts might be avoided. *The Guardian* news-paper reopened the debate in June 1997[3] in anticipation of the release of Graham Seddon, a convicted paedophile, detained for questioning after being found carrying a bag of toys and books and, he admitted to police, 'on the lookout for a child'. *The Guardian* article says, 'the unrepentant sex molester who snatches young children off the streets has become the bogey figure lurking behind the latest moral panic', and describes 'paedophiles' capacity to destabilise communities' as 'not seen since the heretic-hunting of the 17th and 18th centuries'. This, of course, is the last thing that those who care about children and work for their good want. The inevitable backlash would undoubtedly be reticence among law-makers and decision-makers, silence in the media for fear of inciting overreaction, and a return to the days when children were sexually abused in silence and those who could do something about it turned a blind eye.

With this word of warning, though, let us return to the streets of the United States. Because, in fact, most of the 100 000 to 300 000 children who are sexually exploited in the United States each year[4] are abused in the home or sold on the streets. A national report in 1989 revealed that there were 1.3 million runaways and homeless young people living on the streets of the United States. Workers who operate shelters for street children say the numbers have probably increased dramatically since then and that, in Chicago alone, in 1995 they were turning away three out of every four children who sought refuge.[5] According to that same report, 5000 street children die every year of assault, illness and suicide. The rest do whatever they can to survive.

'If the kids don't hook up with some kind of organisation within 72 hours,' Joe Gregersen, of the Church of the Brethren in Chicago, says, 'they'll probably turn to pornography, drugs or prostitution. They'll perform oral sex for a hamburger.'

More than 25 per cent of these children, according to the 1989 report, have run away from home because they were being sexually abused there. Twenty per cent said their parents abused alcohol or drugs. Most of the others cited 'unemployment, family mental health and neglect' as their reasons for escaping to the streets.

On the streets they find a sense of 'family', a sense of community. Although they are exploited by pimps, drug-dealers and other low-life criminals, they are part of a community which also includes other children who have been through the same experiences they have and who daily share the same struggles.

Some of them keep going because they hope that one day they will find a new life away from the streets. Perhaps one of their clients will fall in love with them, turn over a new leaf and marry them. Maybe they will miraculously find a 'regular' job and be able to support the simple lifestyle they dream of. Some of them, though, see no alternatives and claim they like the life they lead. These children call themselves 'gutterpunks' and say they love the 'freedom' life on the streets offers. 'No rules. It's just one big circle – sex, drugs and punk rock,' one of them says. It is frightening to imagine what this young boy must be escaping from.[6]

What goes through the minds of the young people who are forced to sell sex on street corners is unfathomable. Their minds, like their bodies, are hardly their own any more. Hooked on drugs, beaten into submission by pimps, twisted by the need to distance themselves from the acts forced upon them, they lose sight of a world which does not involve degrading themselves many times a night, submitting to tortures too horrific to think about, knowing that tomorrow will bring the same again. 'It's total mind control,' Trevor Townsend, Director of Community Services in Nova Scotia, Canada, told writer Jim Hutchison in August 1994.[7]

Canada, too, has been learning about the children who are sold for sex on its streets. Melissa was one of them. When the 15-year-old brought home four friends she had met outside her school in Vancouver, her mother was pleased she had found boyfriends. One night just a month later, Melissa did not come home from school. When her mother called a school friend of Melissa's to ask where her daughter might be, she learned that the 'boyfriends' were pimps.

One of them, only 18 years old himself, had been taking Melissa out to eat, buying her clothes and promising her love and excitement. He begged her to run away with him and, when she did, he took her to a motel, supplied her with cocaine and ordered her on to the streets to pay off her debts. To keep her submissive, he fed her drugs and beat her. A favourite instrument of torture is the so-called 'pimp stick', a bent coathanger heated to red-hot and then used as a whipping tool.

Eventually Melissa got to a phone and called her mother. The line went dead before they could talk but, when Melissa managed to call again some days later, her mother was ready. She had arranged for a police phone tap and got the address of the motel where her daughter was being held. Melissa's mother now runs a group called Parents for the Protection of Sexually Exploited Children, and says, 'If you don't get the kids back from the pimps within a month, chances are slim you'll get them back at all.' In a new twist, Vancouver police have reported older pimps using 'popcorn' or 'bubble gum' pimps, some as young as 14, to recruit girls at school.

Melissa's story is repeated endlessly across the cities of Canada. Social workers in Toronto estimate there are 10 000 children living on the streets of that beautiful city, and that many of them fall prey to pimps. There are between 600 and 3000 minors involved in the sex trade in Montreal. In June 1996 a paedophile pornography ring was broken up in London, Ontario, and 30 men were charged with more than 1300 counts of sex crimes against more than 50 boys, some as young as eight years of age. More than 400 children – some as young as 11 – are reported as working for pimps in Calgary.

Calgary was once known as Canada's 'sex capital', in the aftermath of the 1988 Winter Olympic Games which brought hundreds of thousands of tourists to the city along with the 'entertainment' they required to round off their winter sports holiday. By 1990, police became aware that organisers of the now dwindling sex trade had introduced a 'new attraction': children. In 1993, the people of Calgary decided enough was enough. They joined together to fight child exploitation in their midst. A police crackdown netted hundreds of pimps. A community-wide awareness campaign alerted children, teachers, parents and everyone else to the dangers of children becoming caught up in commercial sex.

Lawyers, judges, police and social workers were put through awareness training to understand why children might be vulnerable, and how those who are at risk need to be protected rather than victimised. Social programmes were initiated, like Street Teams, a roving group of citizens who help children escape prostitution and who work to disrupt the marketing of them. The rescued children are returned to their families or, if that is not a safe option, to 'created' families. In three years, the number of children enslaved in the sex trade in Calgary dropped by 25 per cent.

The rescued children of Calgary, though, remain a problem. Helping children who have been subjected to sexual exploitation is not easy. 'When a girl has been sexually assaulted hundreds of times,' says Ross McInnes, a retired police officer in Calgary, 'there's a need to help her learn how to go about having a normal date with a 14-year-old boy. How do you go out bowling, or to the zoo? And what does £10 allowance mean to a child who has seen £300 flow through her fingers in one night?'

Into the African continent

On a whirlwind tour of the world to seek out the story of the sexual exploitation of children, it is often just the amounts of money quoted that change. The defining role played by root causes – poverty in some parts of the world, consumer pressures in another, abuse in the family elsewhere, entrapment by criminal gangs – may change in emphasis, but the end results for the children devalued one way or another by the world they live in are the same.

On the streets of Sierra Leone, West Africa, children sell their bodies to foreign soldiers and fishermen for as little as five US cents (3p). They are victims of the country's five-year war and, like so many other children worldwide, but for different reasons, have been cast out on to the streets, where they are expected to feed themselves and survive.

At a 1995 conference in Pretoria, South Africa, a UNICEF representative[8] said that, 'African children, mostly girls but also some boys, are increasingly falling prey to sex tourism, prostitution and rape. Civil wars, poverty and the AIDS epidemic have left millions of African pre-teens and adolescents without a source of income or a stable family environment; many end up selling sex to survive.'

In Sierra Leone, homeless children sell survival sex to Portuguese, Spanish and Russian fishermen. Some 80 per cent of the street children are infected with sexually transmitted diseases. In Angola, girls as young as 12 are reported to offer themselves to visiting foreigners in an attempt to survive following 30 years of civil war in that country in which at least 100 000 children lost their families. A national reunification programme launched by UNICEF in 1991 resulted in only 6000 children being successfully reunited with family members. It is now estimated that more than 1.5 million children live in abject poverty in Angola, which also has the highest child death rate in the world. Ninety-four children under the age of five die every day from curable diseases. There are 4000 children prostituted in the Angolan capital, Luanda, alone.

In 1993, 3202 children were listed as 'official' victims of 'rape and ravishment'. Official figures[9] show a growing trend. The next year the figure had risen to 4114. By 1995 it was higher again: 4164. Most of the rape occurs on the streets of the largest cities, Luanda and Benguela, and is carried out by gangs. 'The offences are preceded by allure, through promises, beguilement and other similar means,' the official report says. Promises. Hope. Dreams. Things that all children have and should have.

'As an effect of the increasing awareness of the fact that children have rights, of the mix of foreigners living temporarily or permanently in Angola, of the migration flux and of the deterioration of the people's social and economic situation, criminalising the commercial sexual exploitation of minors and strongly repressing it within the acknowledged lucrative markets, will introduce new lifestyles and behaviour which will completely alter the picture as described above.' A cryptic prediction from the official government report, which gives no indication whatsoever of how the picture and 'lifestyles' of children will change at all. If anything, the influx of foreigners, deterioration of socio-economic infrastructure and the movement of people from rural to urban areas which will probably result are more likely to put children at greater risk of exploitation.

'It is unofficially known', the report continues, in a double-speak that defies belief, 'that there are special lodgings which house minors over 12 years old, creating the ideal conditions for this flourishing market. Unfortunately, in exceptional cases, some children are there by tacit consent of the parents, tutors or people in charge of minors.

'It is also known that there are minors who leave Angola, accompanied by "well-meaning" persons, whose destiny is uncertain as the Diplomatic Missions do not have necessary means to follow up on these cases. We cannot permit that this calamity persists, or we will be considered accessories.'

It is unthinkable that a report like this could be written and made public; that there could be 'unofficial' knowledge with enough detail to specify the ages of the children and the consent of their guardians; that the report could at the same time list sections of the Penal Code which could be used against 'such perverted behaviour'; that the phenomenon of child prostitution could be so widespread and public that there is even a name for the girls in Portuguese, the official language of Angola: *catorzinhas*, or 'little 14-year-olds'.

The Angolan authorities, though, serve here only as example. They are by no means alone among African countries who, while cursorily acknowledging that 'the problem' exists in their country, do little to fight against it other than list legal instruments already in place (but largely unused), trot out statistics (the colonial legacy of bureaucracy for bureaucracy's sake lending an ironic twist to these meticulously compiled lists), and complain that they could do something about the situation if only they had more money.

In the midst of these excuses, South African President Nelson Mandela spoke out against the commercial sexual exploitation of children in words far removed from the whining pleas of many other governments of Africa.

As a contributory factor to sexual exploitation, poverty cannot be underestimated when we consider that young people are often forced to the streets to make a living, or parents sell their children sexually as a means of income. South Africa will need to pay attention to poverty and other contributory factors in order to make progress towards the prevention and treatment of sexual exploitation and abuse. This will involve legislative action to enhance the protection of children. It will include an increasing focus through a practical programme on gender sensitivity and on the empowerment and protection of women and the girl child. And, in addition to a range of socioeconomic programmes of reconstruction to address issues of poverty, our welfare policy and programme is undergoing transformation. Early childhood development, youth development and comprehensive changes to our child and youth care system are key components of the process. The far-reaching changes South Africa is making to its education system, both for children and adults, will also greatly assist in preventing and addressing the exploitation of children. South Africa is proud to have signed and ratified the United Nations Convention on the Rights of the Child and is currently working towards its full implementation through a comprehensive National Plan of Action for Children. In days gone by, and possibly even today in many instances, the view has prevailed that children should 'be seen and not heard'. The time has come for our children to be seen, and to be very clearly heard. The cries of our abused and exploited children must no longer fall on deaf ears or closed minds.[10]

Let us not be too cynical here. The battle against commercial sexual exploitation of children must begin with a call to arms. It must begin with strong words and outrage. It is a battle that must, as much as anything, be fought with harsh rhetoric and gentle persuasion, because it is a war that has as much to do with perceptions, mindset and attitudes as it does with poverty and hunger. Starving children may need money for food, but they should not have to earn it by selling sex. Middle-class kids in industrialised cities who have turned to drugs may need temporary supplies while society is helping them kick the habit, but they should not have to sell their souls to get them. Let us even admit that ageing businessmen might have a right to excitement, thrills and something 'new' in their lives, but let us never allow that such a right might involve degrading a single child.

So President Mandela's words are welcome, especially in light of the large number of children who today are forced to sell sex to survive in South Africa. Adele du Plessis also speaks out, 'I say to society: Don't point fingers at my kids. You are the scum that buys them. The average client is Mr Upstanding Citizen. It's your nice Mr Jones from next door.'

Adele du Plessis runs a shelter for children forced to prostitute themselves on the streets of Johannesburg.[11] Since 1990, she has handed out advice and condoms to the more than 26 000 children who are sexually exploited each year on the streets of this South African city. Many of her 'clients' are girls of 12. 'They come in for a chat, a peanut butter sandwich and condoms,' du Plessis says. She also tells of the time she had to deal with the case of a sexually abused child brought to her in desperation. The child was nine months old.

Many of du Plessis's children are driven into the sex trade to earn money to live, but many are not. There are girls from South Africa's wealthiest areas, too, forced into prostitution to finance expensive drug habits and to pay the thugs who hold a gun to their heads as they demand payment.

Du Plessis believes harsher punishment is necessary if South Africa's promises to its children are to be kept. 'The laws are pathetic,' she says. 'The kid goes through hell to testify and at the end of the day the guy gets a slap on the wrist.' Recent sentences confirm her fears. A man convicted of raping a three-year-old child in 1995 was sentenced to five years in prison, of which two years were suspended. The child will hardly be in school when the man is back on the streets.

In other instances, South African law enforcement agencies seem to be taking a tougher line. In July 1995, South African police seized computer files containing pornographic images of children as young as six years old. They had been trailing the man accused of possessing the images, a sex offender whose first conviction had been for showing indecent pictures to an 11-year-old girl in an attempt to coerce her into compliance.[12] The South African man was accused of being part of an international child pornography ring which distributed images via the Internet. This crackdown was part of 'Operation Starburst', a coordinated move which also netted porn distributors in Europe, the United States, and Asia.

South Africa still has much to do, though, to dismantle the established and profitable commercial sexual exploitation of children through brothels, pimps and other intermediary exploiters.

Tragically, the child sex trade in South Africa still bears the hallmarks of apartheid. It has been described as 'a mixture of "first" and "third" world', a race- and wealth-oriented system in which well-to-do white and light-skinned coloured girls are kept in high-class brothels to service the needs of predominantly white middle-class men, while black and darker-skinned coloured girls work out of seedy dockland bars and cheap tenement blocks.[13]

The brothels in which children are available in Durban, for example, are often slum tenements where two or three children are kept by a madam. She may find customers by herself or send the girls on to street corners to bring them in, but she is also likely to have a network of taxi drivers, hotel staff and escort agency owners who direct those looking specifically for young children to her. The children have usually run away from home or are street children, so damaged by the physical and mental abuse they have suffered that they have no desire to escape from the madam's 'caring' arms. Police report that, when they do pick up young girls and remove them to safe houses, they often run away and return to the brothels they were kept in. One officer of Durban's Child Protection Unit told O'Connell Davidson of a madam who is renowned among runaway girls for the 'help' she provides. 'They approach her in the hope of securing the paltry material rewards that are otherwise entirely beyond their reach,' the officer said, referring to the drugs, clothes and food the children cannot otherwise obtain. 'She does not need to entice or entrap children in order to commercially sexually exploit them.' Except, of course, that the food they need to survive is itself enticement and entrapment.

In Kenya, too, the prostitution of children is rampant. So much so in fact, that, according to press reports, it has become 'a major tourist attraction'.[14] Both boys and girls are involved in the sex trade in Kenya, although most of the exploited children are girls between the ages of six and 16. They sell sex on the streets of Nairobi, where the city plan is divided into 'turfs', and the gangs of girls that work them are presided over by gangs of boy pimps, with a hierarchical structure that sees a 'senior' pimp as the ringleader.

The gangs not only have a leader, they have a democratic process. They vote on what 'business' they will get into in order to survive. Some choose begging, parking cars for a fee or collecting rubbish. Those who want to make more money trade in children's bodies.

These children – the girls and the boys who live off them – are victims of the breakdown of extended family structures that were once so central to African life. Once, for example, Elizabeth would have been cherished by her family.[15] Now she has been abandoned first by her mother and then by her grandmother. She arrived in Nairobi with her mother who, when she could no longer afford the token fees to send Elizabeth to a government school, left her with her grandmother and returned to the countryside. Elizabeth's grandmother chased her on to the streets. There, she turns tricks for £3 a time but has to give half of that to the gang that controls the streets. Although reports say that drugs are not yet a major factor in the street life of Nairobi, many of the children sniff glue to numb themselves against the indignity of their fate.

The Undugu Society, a private charity that has for some years worked with the street children of the Kenyan capital, estimates that this city of two million inhabitants has several thousand children without parental supervision, and 50 000 more who roam the streets because their parents cannot afford school fees. UNICEF reports that between 40 per cent and 75 per cent of squatter families in Nairobi are headed by single women, 'symptomatic of the breakdown of the traditional family structures and the increasingly ambivalent role of the male in the household'.

Four thousand children are sold for sex on the streets of the Angolan capital Luanda. As many as 26 000 in Johannesburg. Thousands in Kenya and Liberia. More in Ethiopia and Zambia. And yet commercial sexual exploitation of children is a criminal activity, and so mostly hidden from public view. As a result, the true figures must far exceed the estimates we have been able to gather. We have hit just the tip of the iceberg.

It seems, too, that every time we think we have begun to paint a comprehensive picture of the scope and nature of the problem of children being sold for sex, something new comes up and makes us think again. Like a hydra-headed monster that regenerates and multiplies each time it is cut back, the commercial sexual exploitation of children just seems to go on spreading and diversifying.

The children of camp and conflict

In recent years, we have become aware of children being sold for sex, in a number of different situations, in the wake of war and conflict. Sometimes, as well as being taken on as child soldiers, girls and boys are recruited into paramilitary and military contingents to serve as non-combatant personnel. This weighty name in normal circumstances would indicate the cooks, labourers or administrative staff who make the machinery of warfare run smoothly. In this case, however, we are talking about children recruited to provide sex to the soldiers.

Civilian children caught up or, increasingly, targeted by conflict are also at risk of exploitation. There are many reports of young Rwandan girls and boys, for example, being sexually humiliated by being forced to watch their mothers and sisters being raped and tortured before being killed during the massacres that took place in their country in 1994. Often the children were then taken along with the killers for a time and forced to act as sexual outlets before they, too, were killed.

Children who escape such horrors may find themselves 'unaccompanied' – the official term for children who have lost their families in conflict or during flight – and are then at risk of further exploitation from other refugees, even from those distributing aid in refugee camps. In these makeshift towns where there is little food, and children are most vulnerable of all, children have been forced to have sex with those handing out the rations or with refugee men who withhold supplies from them. Before the second outpouring of Rwandan refugees in late 1996, when the camps around Goma were still relatively 'settled', there were more babies being born in the camps than there were refugees returning to their homes. Many of these babies were born to girls as young as 13 and 14, who thus became ever more dependent on hand-outs of food and water.

Caroline Lees travelled to Zaïre for the British tabloid *The Sunday Express* in July 1996. In the Lac Vert refugee camp in Goma, she met Zyira, a 13-year-old schoolgirl who was given a bag of flour by a Zaïrian soldier in exchange for her body, which he took by force. A mother at 13, Zyira then found herself forced to provide sex to soldiers and refugees in the camp in exchange for cooking oil, milk powder and shelter for her child.[16]

The aid agencies working in the camps are powerless to act, warned against 'interfering' in the 'social life' of the camps. As a result, children as young as three and four, separated from their families in the rush to escape massacre in Rwanda, were 'adopted' by adults who hire them out to soldiers for sex.

There seems little point in reminding these exploiters that Article 3 of the *1949 Geneva Convention relative to the Protection of Civilian Persons in Time of War* prohibits 'outrages upon personal dignity, in particular humiliating and degrading treatment' or that Article 77 of the *1977 Protocol relating to the Protection of Victims of International Armed Conflicts* specifically states that 'children shall be the object of special respect and shall be protected against any form of indecent assault'.

Rwanda is perhaps the most recent example of the sexual exploitation of children at work in situations of conflict, but there are others. Following people movements out of Benguela province, Angola, in March 1993, civilians were gathered in centres for displaced people, where the cramped living conditions made exploitation easy. That same year and into 1994, Kuito province was held siege for 16 months by UNITA troops who raped many of the young girls when they were forced to cross the lines to find food.

Children have also been prostituted in refugee and displaced people's camps in Liberia and Guatemala, sometimes by their own families who trade them for food and other basic necessities.

Reports from the war zones of former Yugoslavia provide further examples of how young children's bodies can become a 'spoil' of war. In Bosnia, girls were often separated from the rest of the population during the terrible 'ethnic cleansing' exercises of the early 1990s and carried off by soldiers and raped. Often they were then kept in servitude until they were no longer required. In Croatia, children were kept locked in houses where they could be 'visited' by militiamen.

Of 12 recent case studies prepared on the commercial sexual exploitation of children in situations of conflict,[17] all 12 name armed forces from *all* sides of the conflict as perpetrators of sexual violence and exploitation of children. Some studies mention that non-military personnel also committed rape and exploitation of children. Six of the 12 case studies – Angola, Bosnia, Cambodia, Croatia, Mozambique and Rwanda – point to the presence of United Nations peace-keeping forces as 'having favoured the development of child prostitution' and a seventh study, on Liberia, mentions that the presence of soldiers from the ECOMOG inter-African contingent promoted child prostitution. According to a 1996 discussion paper prepared by Save the Children,[18] in Liberia 'prostitution has changed considerably with the involvement of children; hundreds of young women and girls aged 10 years and above are reportedly loitering around military camps prostituting themselves in pursuit of basic necessities'.

The report points out that traditionally girls in the country tribes of Liberia were married early, at 13 or 16 years of age, in order to ensure their virginity for their husbands. Although early marriage is much less common now that conflict and poverty have forced people to the cities, the practice of sexual initiation at these young ages continues and parents, mostly mothers, encourage young girls to begin sexual activity to obtain money for the family or to find a husband. Such promiscuity remains unacceptable to the large majority of people, however, and most people refuse to consider it as prostitution. They see it rather as a semi-legitimate way of surviving.

The soldiers reportedly use the term 'prostitution' freely, however, and judge the girls accordingly. Within the various militia in the country, drug and alcohol abuse is high, and use of children for sex has increased. The girls rarely use condoms, since they believe that they can 'catch' cancer from them. As a result, they often find themselves with babies of their own and another mouth to feed.

The argument that inappropriate behaviour is to be expected whenever there are large contingents of unaccompanied men far away from home and family and in strange countries with little to do and lots of money to do it, hardly holds water when the case of UN or other international peace-keeping troops is cited. They are not just men, not just soldiers, but first and foremost peace-keepers mandated by the international community to safeguard people whose only hope is that outside forces will protect them and give them a chance to rebuild their lives. That such men might abuse this sacred trust to exploit children is intolerable.

The evidence is clear, however, that in the past this has happened. Most damning of all is an episode meticulously recorded by the International Save the Children Alliance,[19] whose Norwegian arm, Redd Barna, opened an office to carry out relief assistance in Maputo, Mozambique, in early 1988.

Mozambique had been engaged in civil war since 1976 but, in October 1992, the Mozambican Government and the RENAMO guerrilla movement signed a cease-fire agreement. The people of Mozambique – 15.3 million in 1995, of whom 7.2 million were under the age of 16 and 2.8 million were less than five years old – escaped the fighting only to be plunged into the poverty, drought and disruption that followed. The return of almost two million refugees from neighbouring countries and the demobilisation of 80 000 soldiers exacerbated food and accommodation shortages and unemployment, and plunged the country into abject poverty.

When the United Nations sent peace-keepers to Mozambique in 1992 to consolidate the cease-fire and prepare for the first ever general elections (October 1994), there were great hopes that this non-aligned international presence might give Mozambique a chance of stability and, ultimately, the means to attract the donor funds it so badly needed to kick-start its rebuilding development programmes.

The peace-keepers, under the acronym ONUMOZ, became operational in early 1993. They comprised military personnel from Uruguay, Bangladesh, Portugal, Zambia, Italy and Botswana, and were under the direction of the

Special Representative of the Secretary-General of the United Nations in Mozambique, Mr Aldo Ajello.

The Italian battalion of some 800 soldiers, code-named 'Albatroz', was based in the areas of Manica and Sofala. With regular rotations, it is estimated that some 3600 Italian soldiers served as Albatroz peace-keepers between April 1993 and March 1994. Most of them were conscripted men between the ages of 18 and 22. They were, according to Redd Barna, 'ill-prepared with hardly any knowledge of the country, its population, customs and traditions. It also became obvious that the Code of Conduct for UN peace-keeping forces and personnel (let alone the UN *Convention on the Rights of the Child*) was hardly known to the Italian and other troops.'

Manica was an easy posting, and the men had little to do and no way to spend the US$70 (£40) to US$100 (£60) daily allowance they were receiving. These may have been factors in what the Redd Barna report euphemistically describes as 'involving themselves in activities that had nothing to do with their mandate'. The Albatroz contingent got into the child sex trade.

By September 1993 the trade had become so organised that the contingent had appointed a professional military Liaison Officer as a mediator between them and the pimps and girls. The soldiers recruited street children for their domestic work, to shop for them, and to procure black market goods. Some of the girls were as young as 12 years of age. The 'going rate' was US$1 (60p) for sex with a condom and US$1.10 (70p) without. As time went by, the Italian soldiers began to visit Mutare city and Harare in Zimbabwe in search of sex.

Redd Barna staff reported seeing Albatroz soldiers in uniform having sex with minors in and around official UN vehicles parked in the Trade Fair car park in Chimoio. Houses were rented for parties and drunk and drugged girls were taken away by police and families. Girls were recruited directly on school premises and local businesses began to move seriously into the trade themselves, establishing brothels and filling the gaps in availability.

At first, complaints from the International Save the Children Alliance, represented in Mozambique by Redd Barna, prompted little official response. An internal UN enquiry concluded that 'there were no irregularities whatsoever'. Then local and international newspapers got hold of the story, reportedly leaked to them from an official in ONUMOZ headquarters. The world's press descended on ONUMOZ and a Commission of Enquiry was set up.

The months that followed were characterised by threatening phone calls to Redd Barna, intimidation of the staff, anonymous letters, tapped phone lines and press denigration campaigns. ONUMOZ staff who supported the move to ascertain the truth were reportedly harassed by colleagues. It is not difficult to see how all those working in Mozambique - aid workers, UN peace-keepers and other UN personnel – must have felt personally threatened by the can of worms Redd Barna's complaints opened. Not only was the reputation of ONUMOZ at stake, but the credibility of the United Nations peace-keeping operation, the security of UN staff and the vital work undertaken by a range of UN agencies working throughout the country was put at risk.

On 25 February, the Commission reported that it had found that the International Save the Children Alliance had indeed pinpointed a serious problem among some of the military personnel of ONUMOZ. A number of soldiers and civilians were sent home immediately; the entire Italian contingent was withdrawn in April 1994, ostensibly for 'financial reasons'. They were replaced by a contingent from Botswana. The Botswana troops soon gained a reputation for sticking honestly to their mandate, and for the community projects, such as building roads and children's playgrounds, that they undertook. It is evident that thorough, speedy investigation and honest public reporting are much less damaging to any reputation than are denial and secrecy.

This brings us back to the question of institutional responsibility. It is individual men (and sometimes women) who sexually exploit children, not individual Italians or soldiers or peace-keepers, any more than it is Cambodians or teachers or Brazilians or tourists. But many individuals wear a badge that not only identifies the 'pack' to which they belong but which bestows the privileges allowed to that pack – like high daily allowances or a uniform – and which consequently also brings the responsibilities of the pack. The United Nations has a duty, when it hands out the blue berets and white logos which carry the hopes of the world community, to take responsibility for its people, in whatever arm of the organisation they work and in whichever part of the world they are posted.

Across the sands of Arabia

We have almost finished our whirlwind tour of the world, visiting sites of some of the most hideous forms of sexual exploitation of children. We have yet to stop in the countries of the Middle East. Many of the governments in this region would tell us that there is no reason to stop here, because commercial sexual exploitation of children simply does not exist in their countries. By now, however, it should be clear that there are few corners of the world where this horrendous trade in children's bodies has not taken hold. And the countries of the Middle East are no exception.

The exotic tales of Ancient Arabia abound with stories of pashas and sheiks who were serviced by harems of a thousand virgins.[20] As wives grew older, they were not replaced but 'supplemented' with younger versions. The great ruler, it seemed, was not only able and willing to satisfy all his women, he took strength from their youthful vigour. As Ron O'Grady has pointed out, even the Hebrew world of the Bible perpetuates this story. When King David of Israel was old and dying, his servants knew what he needed: 'His servants said unto him, Let there be sought for my lord the king a young virgin; and let her cherish him, and let her lie in thy bosom, that my lord the king might get heat.'[21]

The role of the girl child has in many ways barely changed in some Middle Eastern societies since the days of King David. As in parts of Asia, the girl child is often a second-class citizen, whose role in the family is to serve first her father then her brothers. Her role in the wider community is subservient to that of men and boys. Little wonder, then, that girls come to be looked upon as marketable commodities whose bodies are little more than receptacles for men's sexual urges.

Still the issue of sexual exploitation of children remains a taboo subject. It is hardly talked about at community level and strongly denied by governments. Yet there is no doubt that it exists, in several different forms.

Discrepancies in the distribution of wealth in the Arab world, for example, give rise to the same sorts of rich to poor country sex tourism that also exists in Europe, South America and Asia. Wealthy men from the Gulf States are known to travel not only to Asia and to other 'traditional' sex tourism destinations but also within the Middle East itself, to Lebanon and to Egypt, where in the former a post-conflict breakdown of social values and in the latter, poverty, are factors contributing to the provision of sexual services, including child prostitution.

In the poorer countries of the region, too, children become vulnerable when they are forced to scratch out a living on the streets. Street vendors, delivery boys and shoe-shine children face the same dilemmas that children in South America do: if they can earn much more by spending one hour with a man who propositions them than they can by working for a week on the streets, why hesitate? In Casablanca, Marrakech, Tunis and Cairo, children who live and work on the streets are known to be prey to tourists and local men.

But most of the sexual exploitation of children that takes place in the Arab world happens behind closed doors. Many young girls from the poorer Arab countries, as well as from southern Asia and other regions of 'supply', are recruited as domestic servants. In March 1996, there were 20 000 Sri Lankan women and girls employed as domestic servants in Jordan alone. The International Labour Organisation (ILO) estimates that in 1990 there were 1.2 million female domestic workers – 20 per cent of the total foreign workforce – in the Middle East. The servants are often expected to supply sexual services to the men of the household. Sometimes they are recruited directly for the work, but often they are deceived into such employment, trafficked across borders and trapped by the debts they accumulate when they are transported and given work papers which may or may not be authentic.[22] An August

1995 report by Human Rights Watch/Asia says the majority of complaints by Sri Lankan female domestics to their country's labour bureau related to sexual aggression.

Child brides and under-age sex

A worrying aspect of commercial sexual exploitation of children in the Arab world, too, is the practice of early marriage. Many agencies working with exploited children believe that such practice is little more than an attempt to legitimise child sex. Girls as young as 12 or 13 years of age are married off to much older men in exchange for dowries and gifts for the family, despite the fact that in most countries of the Arab world the legal age for marriage is 18 (16 in Jordan, 21 in Oman and 'puberty' in Saudi Arabia). These girls, wedding bands or not, are no more ready physically or mentally for sex than any other 12-year-old child. Moreover, in countries where early marriage is common, it leads to a general perception of the girl-child as ready for sex, and encourages men who are inclined to seek out children to believe that society is effectively confirming their readiness. In Lebanon, for example, although the age of majority is 18, the legal age for sexual relations is several years younger, which suggests acceptance of the fact that someone other than the child will take responsibility for the child's initiation into sex, presumably a parent or husband. In Saudi Arabia, sexual relations may legally begin upon marriage.

Article 2 of the *United Nations Supplementary Convention on the Elimination of All Forms of Discrimination against Women*[23] stipulates that, 'States Parties undertake to prescribe, where appropriate, suitable minimum ages of marriage, to encourage the use of facilities whereby the consent of both parties to a marriage may be freely expressed in the presence of a competent civil or religious authority, and to encourage the registration of marriages.' Although this Supplementary Convention was ratified by 106 countries, however, a high number of them recorded reservations against their ratification.

Recent research shows that early marriages are becoming more commonplace in some parts of the world, despite legal restrictions. Partly this is because laws in many countries stipulate the age of consent to marriage without parental permission, but allow marriage with parents' permission much earlier. In Yemen, for example, the majority of girls are married between the ages of 12 and 15, despite a 1978 Family Law mandating three years in prison for those involved in the marriage of girls under 16. In the Nizwa area of Oman, 27 per cent of girls are married before the age of 11. In recent years Iran has revoked a 1976 Civil Code specifying a minimum age of 18 and introduced a new minimum age of 13. Legal requirements to verify age, register marriage and confirm both parties' consent can be and are regularly circumvented; in some countries the girl does not even need to be present at the ceremony.

While commentators in the industrialised countries often point to the practice of early marriage as somehow indicative of 'primitive' religious practices, journalists are beginning to uncover examples of such disguised exploitation much nearer home. In January 1996 an Australian magazine[24] carried the shocking story of a community where girls leave school in the afternoon to go home to their husbands and children, clean house, prepare meals, put the kids to bed and then do their homework. These 12- and 13-year-olds, married in some cases to young men but in at least one instance to a septuagenarian, live in a small town in the US state of Kentucky, just 650 kilometres away from the nation's capital, Washington. 'You have to understand that people here don't have a lot of exposure to other people,' the school principal is quoted as saying. 'The family may think it's more respectable for their daughters to be married. They're afraid that if they don't let them get married, they will ruin their name – in other words, get pregnant and be unwed.' As a result, girls as young as 12 find themselves living both an 'adult' life – with husband, children, debts, housework, responsibilities – and the life of a child with all it entails: school, expectations from parents and siblings, peer pressures. It is little wonder that many of these childhood marriages end early, and that many of the girls grow up without a normal education, with children to care for but no means of earning an income, relying on food stamps and welfare payments to survive.

What works to some extent against the expansion of commercial sexual exploitation of children in the Middle East, however, is the Islamisation that several countries have undergone in recent years. Despite western perceptions that girls and women are ill served by Islam, in fact Shari'a law provides a degree of protection to the girl-child and the woman, for example by suppressing the use of pornography. Shari'a law states that it is woman's duty not to provoke male lust, and by this pornography depicting women and girls is effectively outlawed. Civil codes are based on Shari'a law and consequently most countries in the Arab world have comprehensive laws against pornography, with penalties ranging from two to 20 years' imprisonment for citizens and immediate deportation for foreigners.[25]

While Islamisation does seem to have inhibited the growth of this form of sexual exploitation of children in the Middle East, however, there are real fears that growing economic imbalance both within this region and globally, the opening up of borders and easier and cheaper travel, and the supply-led sex trade organised by criminal networks who move children across borders and fuel demand, will gradually lead to an increase, if not in children being exploited within the region, then to travellers from the region seeking sex with children in neighbouring countries.

The spinning globe we have travelled, then, is coloured with the suffering of our children. Although the colours may vary in intensity and there may be varieties in the hues, all the countries of the world are painted in the same colours and from the same palette. These paints are in the hands of grown-ups but, before we try to see the face of the painter, it is time to look in more detail at the factors that make his work easier: the root causes of commercial sexual exploitation of children.

3 Tightening the noose: How children are trapped into sex

Why do some children become trapped in the hideous trade of child sex while others do not? Once upon a time, many people would have answered, 'poverty is to blame'. That belies the fact that millions of families worldwide live in abject poverty yet their children play in freedom.

The story is told by aid workers in India of flights over villages along the India/Nepal border in which the families who have sold their children into sex can easily be identified: their homes have brand new roofs. Why is it that, in the same village, some parents will hand over their child to a pimp in exchange for the money to buy a new roof, while neighbours in the same village will go without a roof over the heads rather than sell a beloved child?

What is at play is what Professor Vitit Muntarbhorn has called 'the poverty-plus factor'.[1]

Poverty and the family

There is no doubt that all people seek for themselves and their families the basic necessities of life: food, water, clothing and a roof over their heads. In some parts of the world, even as the new millennium draws close, these are extremely difficult to obtain, not only because some countries absolutely are poor but also because some countries choose to direct what wealth they do have away from basic necessities into the purchase of arms, or to otherwise distribute wealth unevenly. As a result, families scrape together just enough to survive. Any further strain on their ability to cope can push them over the edge and lead to a situation where desperation sets in. Such strains might include losing the family breadwinner through disease, war or migration, losing the home through conflict or flight, or a hike in the price of basic food-stuffs following a natural disaster or civil war. Some families will not survive. Others might well, at the very end of their tether, sell a child into slavery.

Some families, although they are pushed to hand over their children in desperation, do not know that the child will enter the sex trade. They are fooled by unscrupulous recruitment agents who promise a better life for the child as a domestic servant, or in other forms of child labour in the big city. The agent hands over money as a 'loan' against the child's eventual earnings, and the child is led away. That is the last the family will see of the child in whom they have put their hope. She – for in this form of recruitment it is usually a girl-child – will be sold on to a pimp or madam, and will then usually be sold several times more as her value diminishes with the loss of virginity and freshness. The child becomes nothing more than a traded good, marked down at bargain basement prices as her health deteriorates, customers lose interest in her and her beauty fades. Long after she has become accustomed to the slavery of commercial sex, she will still be paying off the 'loan' her parents received on that distant, hopeful day when she began her 'new life'.

Another 'plus' that works hand-in-hand with poverty to put children at risk is the increasing breakdown of the family. As people move from country areas to big cities, or across borders in search of economic opportunities, they leave behind extended family networks which once would have helped them through. Often the men of the family leave the women and children behind, and they may fall prey to recruiters who threaten violence or, quite simply, steal the children. New city dwellers, too, find that the push of modern life, presuming they can survive in their new surroundings, means that they work longer hours, away from home, and their children spend more time alone on the streets, again at the mercy of pimps and recruiters, drugs or clients who offer much-needed money.

In this climate of survival-at-all-costs, the girl-child is particularly vulnerable. Families who have arrived from rural areas and traditions might have several children – more usual in the country where couples will have children to help work the land, and to compensate for high infant death rates. In the city, such large families are a drain on scarce income and space, and it is not unknown for families to 'shed' a child so that the others can eat. A girl-child is sold or pushed on to the streets, since she has less value than a boy-child. There she is completely alone and knows that she is unwanted and unloved. Or, if the family is prepared to live with the knowledge of the source of her income, she may simply be put to work in the sex trade to bring home money for the family. There are reports of older sisters entering the commercial sex trade 'willingly', to prevent younger siblings from being forced to sell themselves. In such cases, as in the vast majority of situations where children are prostituted, the concept of 'willingness' must be understood as force by circumstance, if not by other people.

'Shamefully,' Vitit Muntarbhorn writes, 'the rights of a child may be violated because he or she is viewed as a factor of production, as an investment for economic returns, rather than as an entity vested with substantive rights and inherent dignity.'

In countries struggling for economic growth, sectors such as tourism and entertainment are often the first to be developed, and this is a 'plus' that can also increase the child's vulnerability. Tourism opens the door to foreigners looking for 'a good time' and, as formal and informal entertainment businesses grow, children can be sucked into them. Often, too, these businesses introduce alcohol, drugs and a confusion of cultural values that can encourage behaviour that would otherwise be unacceptable in the community.

There is also no doubt, though, that some families who sell their children into the commercial sex trade do so willingly. They have less concern for the child than they do for the goods and services they can purchase with the money she earns or the lump sum they receive when they sell her. As technology breaks down international borders and advertising opens up new possibilities to people who once would not even have known they existed, there is an irresistible push to buy, rent, possess. In countries of the so-called Third World, this may be as simple as wanting to own a radio. In the developed world it might be the overwhelming 'necessity' of a second car, a newer model refrigerator or some electronic gadget the neighbour has that suddenly seems indispensable. It is inconceivable to most of us, but some parents will look at their child, consider what they could do with the money they could get if they sold her, and seek out the best deal they can get.

In a world where a child has less value than a new refrigerator, it is not surprising that some parents also abuse their children sexually at home. It is just a body, after all. Just a receptacle for sex. Hardly a human being. Something you can trade in for an item you want more.

Non-commercial sexual abuse in the home is often itself a contributory factor to children entering the commercial sex trade. Imagine a young girl of 14 or 15 who has been violated by her father or by another male relative over and over for two or three years already. How does she feel about her body? Is it something she cherishes, wants to take care of? Or is it something she hates above all else, the outer case of her very essence but so abused, so dirty, so despicable that she might as well offer it on street corners to anyone who is stupid enough to pay her for it? These are the sentiments often expressed by young people who sell sex on the streets of Europe, South and North America, Africa and elsewhere.

Such children are also often described as 'selling themselves voluntarily' or 'becoming child prostitutes by choice'. It is a sick world that puts the blame for such prostitution on the children who might well have chosen not to enter the sex trade if they had not been abused and demeaned by those they expected to love and cherish them.

The image of the child

The despicable message that the body of a child is a worthless receptacle for others to pay for and play with, is a message that comes not only from sexual abuse in the home but also indirectly from the images we paint of our children in the media.

There was controversy in Great Britain in mid-1996 when a 12-year-old schoolgirl was signed up by a well-known modelling agency and was shown in sensuous poses in a British daily newspaper. This public mix of sex and childhood caused a great deal of soul-searching in the press and among the public, and even the child's mother admitted that there was a 'sexual angle' to the poses in which her daughter had been photographed. Psychologist Dorothy Rowe told the *Daily Mail* newspaper, 'There is something intriguing about the young girl who is just discovering life and is beginning to wonder what it's all about. It is the kind of titillation in which a virginal girl intrigues a man. In areas of sexuality intended to intrigue, it is especially dangerous because the child is being presented with issues that they are not really ready to deal with, no matter how precocious they look.'[2] It is not only children who are confused by this mix of sex and childhood, of course; this message may also be received by those who are looking for ways to justify their own tendencies to see childhood and sex as going hand-in-hand. Paedophiles already have a checklist of reasons why their behaviour is not inappropriate; this might well seem the ultimate community seal of approval.

While the use of 12-year-old models in sexy adult poses is still not common in fashion magazines or other forms of advertising, the advertising media have come under heavy criticism for using more and more adult models who *look like* children. Small-breasted, underdeveloped adult women with makeup, hairstyles, clothes and poses that might generally be classified as 'child-like' also contribute to blurring the line between child and adult, between too young for sex and sexually mature. 'The woman-child ... rules the catwalk.'[3]

In May 1996 Swiss watch manufacturer Omega announced that it was withdrawing advertising from *Vogue*, one of the world's most important fashion magazines, because of the use of child-like models. Within weeks, Omega had received strong messages of support and a barrage of free publicity, despite the withdrawal of its threat by chairman Nicolas Hayek. Still, Omega brand director Giles Rees wrote to *Vogue*, 'I would hope that the tremendous support and encouragement that we have received from the media and particularly from the public would urge you to consider addressing these issues with your editorial staff.'

The trend does not seem to be changing. Music videos, movies, advertising billboards, posters, magazines – a whole range of media which have a major impact on both children and adults and which might make an enormous contribution to protecting the rights of the child and to helping people of all ages understand nascent sexuality, the value of the child, the value of sex and how to avoid confusing the two and falling into the trap of under-age commercial sex – continue in many countries to push the limits of responsibility.

There was public outcry in Europe in early 1996 at an American film, *Kids*, which some critics condemned as voyeuristic. The film, which dealt with under-age sex, amongst other things, featured amateur actors engaging in violent sex. Many believed that the actors themselves were under the age of consent, and expressed fears both that the young actors were being exploited and that young people in the audience might consider them as role models.[4] In some countries, the film was given an 'adults only' certificate, although that is not, in itself, a guarantee that minors will not see it.

Such negative images of children and sex need to be considered in the context of enormous changes in the child's viewing and reading habits. In today's world, fewer children watch television or go to the cinema with parents and adult supervisors. Whereas once parents might discuss media images with their children, balance them with other, differing images, and offer guidance and support as children deciphered the images they saw, nowadays parents often do not even know what their children are watching or reading. Advances in technology mean that children can record films and watch them when parents are not at home, rent videos, access images on their computer screens. A *Sunday Times* survey in late 1996 found that children as young as nine in the UK were regularly watching sexually explicit and violent videos, often, although not always, without the knowledge of their parents. Many of the children watched videos with groups of friends and reacted to peer pressure to watch certain kinds of videos.[5]

While parents blame the media for producing images they would prefer their children not to see, the media blame parents for not taking responsibility for keeping their children away from images they feel unsuitable for them. In reality, of course, media and parents have to share responsibility for the images that are produced and the access children have to them. Rightly, however, parents win the argument that, if media companies did not produce the unsuitable images in the first place, then the question of access would never even arise.

This is the reasoning that has been used to argue strongly about a 1996 remake of the film of Vladimir Nabokov's novel, *Lolita*, first published in English in Paris in 1955. This is the story of 12-year-old Dolores Haze, a precocious girl who seduces her mother's middle-aged lodger, Humbert Humbert, and runs away with him. Their ill-matched liaison does not last, of course, and Lolita leaves Humbert for Quilty, a manic, twisted procurer who introduces her to a group of 'bohemian' colleagues interested in making pornographic films. Eventually Lolita escapes, marries a boring young man and has a baby. Humbert tracks down Quilty, kills him and ends his days in prison.

It sounds a rather glib story when stripped back to skeletal plot like this, but *Lolita* has been raised to the ranks of classic literature partly because of the riskiness of its subject-matter, partly through Nabokov's literary skills which go beyond subject and brilliantly marry psychology, humour and lyricism, and partly thanks to an excellent 1962 film starring British actor James Mason as Humbert and a child actress named Sue Lyons who brought to the part of Lolita a steaming voluptuousness that was at once child-like and terrifyingly evil.

Nabokov's book was already controversial, given its paedophilic subject-matter, but the film caused uproar. Hollywood columnist Louella Parsons considered it so filthy 'it made me want to take a bath'. It was considered 'a threat to world morality'. Mason's Humbert was not the manipulative paedophile Nabokov had created, but a hesitant, likeable, intelligent man somewhat led astray. The screen Lolita, on the other hand, was entirely without morality, using sex to lure Humbert, use him and then cast him aside. In the tradition of Dostoevsky's young heroines, who surprise with their sexuality and 'availability',[6] Lolita showed an intention to seduce that movie-goers found shocking in the extreme. People were outraged that such a message could be brought to the screen. Lyons herself has claimed that playing Lolita left her with psychological stresses from which she never recovered. Lolita went on to 'leave the realms of fiction and enter the language as a term of salacious disapproval'.[7]

In 1996, the Lolita debate reopened, when the novel was reinterpreted in a film remake by director Adrian Lyne. Amid much public criticism of the explicit sex scenes and inadvisability of releasing the film in the wake of a number of highly publicised child sex scandals, press reports were less than favourable. 'This film has been made for shock value,' one article suggested, with barely disguised irony. '[The young actress's] concerned mother will surely bank the cheques in a high-interest savings account and prevent her daughter from watching the end result until she is older.'

Such cynicism underplays the real concerns many people have that adult men looking for an excuse to exploit children will watch a film like *Lolita* and find the rationale they are seeking. Or that children confused by the barrage of messages the media are sending, with few support mechanisms at home or in the community and at risk from an ever-increasing demand for under-age sex, might come to believe the lesson that 12-year-olds do have sex with old men and live happily ever after.

Children form their values, though, not only from media images that deal explicitly with those values. They also learn what adults think of them indirectly from the pictures of children that adults paint. The attitude of the media to adolescence itself contributes to young people's image of themselves and their place in society. MTV, the television music channel aimed at young people and which has been called 'the young people's equivalent of the newspaper', features a successful duo of cartoon characters who go by the names 'Beavis and Butthead'. These two-dimensional adolescents are every mother's nightmare. They have half a brain between them and do not know how to use it. They skip school, listen only to heavy metal rock music, blow green slime from their noses and make obscene noises and gestures. They enjoy titillation television with big breasts and sleazy sex. They are mindless, grotesque, stomach-churning morons. And they are loved by young people in all the countries where MTV is shown. They feature on T-shirts, in books, on mugs as icons of youth and, in 1997, featured in their own full-length feature film.

Despite a rather tongue-in-cheek disclaimer at the beginning of each programme that Beavis and Butthead are only cartoon characters and not intended to be seen as role-models, their brainless way of talking, buzz-words and catch-phrases pepper the speech of the adolescents who wear their gormless faces on their chests. In a world where so many of the images young people receive are two-dimensional, and the boundaries between reality and media message are increasingly difficult to define, children are taking Beavis and Butthead much more seriously than their creators intended.

So what is television saying to young people who watch Beavis and Butthead? We cannot be sure. It is to be hoped that, in as many homes as possible, young viewers are groaning and laughing at the pair, taking them at face value and sharing with their parents a loathing of all the twisted life values these two empty-heads share, in other words working out for themselves where the fantasy of cartoon adolescence ends and the reality of life begins. Disconcertingly, though, it is likely that in many homes less protected adolescents are imbibing the values of Beavis and Butthead and, in the process, becoming even more confused about where they fit in to this exceedingly complex world. The international news magazine *Newsweek* carried this comment from MTV's Abby Terkuhle on Beavis and Butthead's 'international stardom': 'I guess it just goes to show that stupidity is universal.' So much for adults' views of children.

Bad attitudes, twisted values

The contribution of media images to the debate on sexual exploitation of children falls into the category 'attitudes and values'. This is the grey area where so many commentators on child sex feel uncomfortable.

When we look at the reasons why children find themselves in the sex trade, it is easy to point the finger at poverty, wars, economic imbalances, breakdown of family. You can write these things down, describe them, calculate them, sometimes even take photographs of them. It is much more difficult to accept that what might underlie the issue of children being sold for sex is the attitude we have towards our children, and our personal values towards sex, responsibility, criminality, right and wrong.

How can we measure what we feel about a child? We might say, 'I love my child and would do anything to protect her from sexual exploitation.' But if we found ourselves stripped of basic necessities, desperate for the next meal, knowing that death surely awaited us and that the old lady at the door offering us money as a loan against our daughter's future earnings in the city might not necessarily be a pimp's intermediary, how many of us would stretch out a hand and take the money? What if we read in the newspaper that a gang of juvenile drug-pushers and pimps has been operating in the neighbourhood, and notice that our 14-year-old son is spending more and more time out late at nights, seems to be too tired to go to school and has extra money for computer games? How many of us would be immediately willing to face the possibility that our child had been trapped into sex and drugs, face him with the thought, suffer the months of fighting at home while the child is grounded, tolerate the accusations of unfairness, the doubts that we might be wrong and the knowledge that we are dealing with something that hits at the core of our relationship with our children? Would it not be easier to give the child the benefit of the doubt and say nothing?

In the closing sessions of the Stockholm Congress in August 1996, a group of young people who had worked on the streets of their cities, who had escaped the sex trade and were now helping others to escape, told of their experiences. There was hardly a dry eye in the room when they had finished. How many of these adult tears, though, were shed for the children themselves, and how many welled up from the guilt that we feel as adults, parents, citizens of this world ultimately unsure of our own attitudes towards children and the values by which we live? When a newspaper reporter asked one of the young people what she thought might be the answer to sexual exploitation of children, she did not hesitate: 'I wish you loved us more,' she said.

Such a cry from the heart becomes a scream of horror in the face of stories like that reported by Agence France Presse on 9 November 1996.[8] The wires that day carried the story of nine adults from the same family in Calais arrested on charges of rape of their own children, nephews and nieces. Between 16 and 23 children, in all, mostly under the age of 15, were 'incited to debauchery' by the adults of their family: five couples and, incredibly, the 60-year-old grandmother, were accused of 'raping children by introducing objects into them'. Although the wire service report also detailed the extreme poverty of the family and their miserable life in caravans with no running water or electricity, this is no justification, no reason, no explanation even of why mothers and fathers, aunts and uncles, grandmothers should subject children who look to them for protection and guidance to the most vile forms of exploitation.

All over the world, in whatever circumstances we live, we need to learn to value our children more than we do. The high value we put on them must be reflected in the way we depict them and reflect their concerns in the media, in the way we teach them – directly and indirectly – about the values we want our world to live by, values relating to issues such as sex, drugs, relationships, honesty, responsibility. We have to help children to draw the lines which define their own set of values, so that they know when they are overstepping that line, and they recognise when others try to pull them across it.

The British actor Roger Moore, famous as the suave hero James Bond and the courageous man-about-town The Saint, has spoken passionately about the need to know the limits we are prepared to accept and where we can stretch them without harming our children. As UNICEF's Special Representative for the Film Arts, he has not only campaigned vigorously for the rights of children to have the food, health, education and security they need to be able to build a life for themselves, he has also spoken critically of those whose work underpins the values of society, urging them to take responsibility for helping to set the limits which protect children from value-driven abuse. He has called this 'art with responsibility': 'Surely we can't accept', Moore has said, 'that the dignity, childhoods, maybe even lives of thousands of children might be sacrificed for the sake of art without responsibility?'[9]

This battle, though, is a tough one. In many societies, the very word 'limits' sends commentators into paroxysms of panic and brings out civil liberties groups, freedom of speech proponents and others who fear that limits are the first step on the road to slavery and dictatorship. Such people should take comfort in the fact that those who work on behalf of children who are in sexual slavery, for the rights of those who are at risk of exploitation and, indeed, for children everywhere, also believe fundamentally in liberty, democracy and freedom of speech. There is a growing belief, however, that for these sacred values to be preserved, those who fight for them should accept the need to draw lines around them beyond which we shall not wander. Beyond the borders of freedom lies a land where children are buggered to death.

Setting the limits

One group that would like to see limits set is Folkaktionen mot Pornografi, the People's Organisation against Pornography, a Swedish group that campaigns for reform of Sweden's liberal pornography laws.

Sweden is the only country in Western Europe which does not prohibit child pornography under either a specific law or a general law covering both adult and child pornography.[10] Legislation against pornography disappeared altogether in 1971 when the Violation of Discipline and Morality Act was abolished. A committee had been set up in 1965 to look at the 'limits of freedom of speech', and concluded that the Act should go, but that limits should be drawn at child abuse and violence. Public opinion surveys concurred, but the Minister of Justice, Lennart Geijer, did not. He said, 'In questions which need to be weighed up carefully we sometimes have to accept things we consider improper and tasteless and which we personally would want to prohibit. That we, despite this, accept such things in for example the media, is the price we have to pay for an extensive freedom of speech and freedom of the press. I do not consider what is suggested in this government bill to be a very high price for safeguarding freedom of speech and freedom of the press.' As Folkaktionen mot Pornografi has pointed out, the 'very high price' he spoke of was the dignity and rights of children not to be sexually exploited.[11] The Act was scrapped without limits.

For the next ten years, child pornography was perfectly legal in Sweden. It was distributed openly until 1980, when the tide of opinion had turned sufficiently for new laws to be enacted. The new Child Pornography Act made the production and distribution, but still not the possession, of child pornography illegal. Thus began what has been called 'the great silence'. For more than ten years, there was little public discussion of child pornography in Sweden. It still circulated, since possession was not a crime, but in close-knit or loosely structured groups and clubs which advertised through men's magazines. Most importantly, the law was very loosely enforced, with most members of the public reluctant to report experiences of seeing child pornography and the police claiming that they did not have the capacity to track down perpetrators. Since possession is not illegal, it is not simply a matter of arresting the person who has the video but tracing where it came from in the first place. And those who are found in possession of child pornography are hardly going to help trace the distributors or producers, since they themselves are potentially implicated. 'People even call me saying they have a child pornography film and ask me if they are allowed to have it, and I have to say sure,' Detective Inspector Lars Lundin, who has worked extensively on the issue, complained to the *Bangkok Post*[12] newspaper.

Amid calls from Interpol, the Committee of Ministers of the Council of Europe, the Nordic Council and the UN Commission for Human Rights, Sweden continues to hesitate. Her Majesty Queen Silvia of Sweden joined the debate in July 1996 when, in a television interview, she spoke out against child pornography and criticised Sweden's politicians for not doing more to end the commercial sexual exploitation of children by pornography makers and users. She suggested that the 349 deputies should see the horrors of child pornography with their own eyes, as she had. 'It is so repulsive,' Queen Silvia had said earlier in 1996, 'it is horrible, unbelievably horrible.' A group of parliamentarians who did watch a five-minute videotape of child pornography showed them by child rights activist Helena Karlen were so distressed that one of them became physically ill and had to be taken away in an ambulance.

A telephone hot-line set up by the Swedish daily *Expressen* for Swedes to call in on this contentious issue received a record number of calls in support of the Queen's stance. But the Swedish freedom of speech lobby is powerful and has strong support. As *The Economist* explained, 'Debauchery behind closed doors, Swedes tend to believe, is a victimless peccadillo. Banning child smut without infringing other liberties is a balance Sweden is finding hard to strike.'[13]

The point that most freedom of speech campaigners seem to ignore is that child pornography is not art, not images, not an expression of freedom. It is *a record of a criminal act being committed*, just as if someone was recording, distributing and watching films of your house being broken into, shops being robbed, women being raped, men being murdered. What child pornography destroys, according to American law professor Catherine MacKinnon, is 'the ability to see that violence ... is violence. Pornography transforms violence into sex.'[14] Folkaktionen mot Pornografi argue that the filming of sexual abuse of children should be regarded not as pornography but as the record of a sexual offence and so should fall under sex crime legislation. Possession and distribution, including import and export, might still need to be regulated under child pornography legislation, but production of child pornography must be recognised as a sex crime, not a question of proper or improper art. This perception argument is important, because Sweden at the moment treats pornography as pictures, rather than recorded events, messages or tools for corruption. A fundamental shift in this perception will be needed to convince those who see the criminalisation of child pornography as a threat to freedom of speech to change their minds.

Until that happens, children and adults will continue to formulate their personal value systems and morality in the context of societies where they can see pornographic videos like *Italian Lolita*, whose cover offers this message:

> Sandy is the cutest, sweetest little girl I have ever met. I am like a father to her. I guess I should take her to the zoo and things like that, but instead I fling her into THIS! Everyone gets to shag the girl. Four masked madmen do it, as do two Africans, and eleven men are having a gangbang with her. All in all, thirty men enjoy themselves with the young girl, complete strangers picked up from the street. It could have been YOU ... Enjoy teenage sex!

The debate on values and the setting of limits has to continue. As it does, it is as well to remember that 191[15] countries have signed and ratified the *United Nations Convention on the Rights of the Child*. Under the Convention, our governments – we – are bound to consider one thing above all others: the best interests of the child. As Folkaktionen mot Pornografi have said, '... raise the question: Whose interests are protected by the law? And who benefits from the silence?'

Much more than local colour

These same questions might be asked in other parts of the world where folk customs, traditional cultures and religious practices also work against the best interests of the child. We have already seen how the Cambodian view of women as 'cloth' compared to men as 'gold', for example, and the reliance on prostitute use that results from this skewed definition of the woman as no more than a receptacle for men's sexual urges, is a major contributing factor to the commercial sexual exploitation of children. There are many more examples, across the world, but perhaps the most striking examples come from Africa and India.

The village of Kuku Ka Bas, in the Alwar district of Rajasthan, is one of many where the men sell their women. The tribe that settled this village, the Rajnats, gave its name to the ancient art of *nautch* dancing which, in the days of the Raj, was a form of entertainment for rajahs and minor princes. Early British settlers looked upon the *nautch* dance as 'an elaborate and polite entertainment', although there is little doubt that some of them, at least, were aware that it was essentially a means of showcasing the girls who were available to the royal audience for sex if their whim dictated.[16]

The customers may have changed but the Rajnat men continue the fantasy. 'Our girls start training when they are about 13,' Mitthu Ram, one of the elders, told a reporter from *The Guardian* newspaper. 'They are taught to dance, and they are sent outside [i.e. to lose their virginity] when they are 18 or 20.' The reporter cut through the niceties of the *nautch* traditions: 'In fact,' he wrote, 'the art of the *nautch* has been reduced to simple, brutish whoring. The last remnant of tradition is *Nath Turai*, the ceremony which accompanies the girl's first night with a paying customer. Some in Kuku Ka Bas claim that this transaction nets up to 20 000 rupees [about £480]. Like so much else in the testimony of the people here, this is almost certainly fantasy. Local reporters say that Rajnat and other tribal virgins – almost always younger than 18 – can be hired for as little as 500 rupees [less than £12]. After that, the girl will be available for as little as 50 pence.'

The girls from Kuku Ka Bas service the needs of businessmen from Delhi and Haryana State, as well as passing lorry drivers, visitors to the district and local men. Although the girls generally remain in the village, some families hope they might 'graduate' to Bombay or Calcutta, from where they will supposedly send home money. In fact, by the age of 18, many of them have already been taking one or two customers a day, may have a child and are likely to be seropositive, since the girls are largely illiterate and have never heard of AIDS or safe sex. The local police, in keeping with their 'customs', are reported to extort money from clients in return for silence, and to demand regular monthly payments from the girls.

UNICEF estimates that 30 per cent of girls sold into sex in the Rajnat tribe are between the ages of 11 and 16.[17]

There are other tribes in India who organise what is loosely called 'rural prostitution', rooted in the exploitation of castes and tribal children, and often containing the trappings of Hinduism. The Devadasi system is another form of ritualised prostitution of children, characterised by traditional Hindu myth and ritual. It is exemplary of a number of religious traditions in which young girls are coerced by family and community to offer their virginity to the gods. In reality, of course, such sexual communion is never divine; it is the adult man who is the god's representative among us who deflowers the virgin girl, in a ceremony that is entirely earth-bound. The spirals of incense smoke and perfumed embers might rise to the heavens, but the child and the man stay on solid ground. In some of these religious rituals, the girl is then expected to return to daily life with only her virginity demolished. Sometimes, however, the fact that the girl is no longer a virgin means that she is obliged to marry soon after her sacrifice, for fear of otherwise being despoiled. Thus she becomes someone else's sex toy. In other cases, the fact that the girl is no longer a virgin may mean that she is now expected to service other men, often for a price set by her family. And in yet other rituals, she may be expected to remain as a servant to the god, housed in the temple brothel where she will keep her body ready for the priests and visitors who claim her in the name of religion.

In September 1996, the Anti-Slavery Society of Australia released a report claiming that some 35 000 virgin girls as young as eight in Ghana, Benin, Togo and Nigeria had been given to 'fetish priests' who treat them like serfs and often rape them.[18] The report explained that, where once the girls had been offered as human sacrifice to ensure success in war, they were now taken into slavery to appease the gods and atone for the wrongdoings of relatives, usually men.[19] The girls, known as *trokosi*, bear two or three children to their priest masters before being released, usually after three to five years. Their 'indenture' excludes them from education, so that they have no way to support themselves when they are freed. In fact, many of the girls stay with the priests since they have no alternative way to live; the report tells of one 86-year-old woman who had lived in slavery her entire life. The Ghanaian Government has said that it believes the practice of 'fetish slavery' is a violation of the constitutional rights of the children, but it is difficult to stop. 'We have to be careful to contain the problem within our own borders,' Betty Akuffo-Amoabeng told *The Times* reporter, 'or parents will simply take their children to neighbouring countries to give them to priests. Then there will be no chance of getting them back.'

There is thus some truth in the belief that 'cultural values' can also contribute to commercial sexual exploitation of children, although such practices
should not be confused with the simple fact of being from another culture. It
is important to make this point because so many sex tourists equate 'foreign-
ness' with 'available for sex' and justify their exploitation on the grounds that
it is 'part of the culture' in the country they are visiting. Moreover, although
culture may be a factor in sexual exploitation of children, it is never a good
reason. There is no good reason why a child should ever be used for sex.

Surfing through Cyberspace

In another time and place from the tribal villages of India, other cultures are
sexually exploiting children on the altars of technology. The closing years of
the twentieth century have brought advances in communications technology
that could only have been dreamed of a decade ago. Adults and children
throughout the industrialised world can now speak to each other across
borders, exchange messages and video clips, join in discussions on a range of
items and share thoughts, ideas, words and pictures via their home
computer. This is the era of Cyberspace. Global communication. Global
exploitation.

'Pair sentenced for selling child pornography via computer', ' Paedophile
shut off from Internet access', 'Sex tourists visit R. via cyberspace', 'Internet
pornography to face crackdown', 'CompuServe will allow sex chats',
'Internet, who should censor whom?', 'Paedophile networks on Internet'.[20]
Newspaper headlines. The old-fashioned way of getting your message
across. In the late 1990s, if you want to talk real-time to potentially 40 million
people across the globe, you hook up your modem, fire up your computer
and dial up the Internet.

This worldwide system of linking personal and business computers to
form a colossal network of users who can speak to each other via electronic
mail, participate in 'bulletin board' and 'newsgroup' discussions, and contribute materials that other users can download through telephone lines into
their own computers, is the stuff dreams are made of. It opens up gigantic
vistas of accessibility to useful, life-enhancing and maybe even life-saving
information. It breaks down borders which once stood in the way of progress
and it gives a voice to many people – including children, who are so much
more comfortable with advanced technology than many grown-ups – who
may once have been doomed to silence.

Tragically, as the newspaper headlines show, it is also open to abuse by
those who seek to sexually exploit children.

Robert Copella was a successful business executive in Chicago when he
met Pamela Kneeland, an Illinois prostitute who was in the Windy City

trying to earn enough money to feed her six-year-old son and also her crack cocaine addiction. They moved in together and set up a business in a city on the Mexican border, selling child pornography by computer. When they were arrested by United States police, they had 1500 images of child pornography scanned into the hard disk of their computer. 'Each of these images ... represents the degradation of a child, some of whom were placed in sadistic and painful situations,' Assistant US Attorney Donna Krappa said during Copella and Kneeland's trial. They were convicted and sentenced to five and a half years and 18 months in jail respectively.

The transmission of child pornography via the Internet is relatively inexpensive and very effective. Pictures can be scanned and video clips can be captured into a computer without any loss of quality in the images; these files can then be attached to electronic mail messages and sent to computers anywhere in the world. Digital cameras cost less than US$100 (£60) in the United States; colour scanners around US$200 (£120). A video capture device which will take pictures directly from a home video camera or video playback machine costs less than US$150 (£90).[21]

Once the pornographic images are computer-ready, they can be sent anonymously using 'anonymous remailers'. These receive messages, remove the address of the sender and then forward them to the next destination. If this is a second anonymous remailer, or third, or fourth – each time in a different country – the origin of the message and pornographic attachments becomes almost impossible to trace. Or at the very least beyond the technical competence and resources of most police forces. Moreover, there are now 'encryption' devices available which allow pornographers to code the message files so that only those who know the code can read them.

In this way, the Internet is being used by paedophiles to make contact with each other and by exploiters to transmit pornographic images, generally home-made, around the world. An exploited child is potentially re-exploited a hundred times in many different countries, by many different clients, and at the moment law-makers and police have not found a way to stop it.

The major hurdle law-makers have to overcome is the transnational nature of the Internet. Where exactly is the law being broken? Is it by the person who uploads the pornographic materials on to the Internet superhighway? By the company that provides the Internet connection, the so-called 'service provider'? By the person who downloads the images into a receiving computer? And are the images covered by pornography laws while they are still on screen, 'floating in Cyberspace', or do they have to be printed into hard copy before they 'become' pornography?

These questions have not yet been answered, and attempts to formulate laws against pornography on the Internet differ from one country to another. The Penal Code (Penal Code Art. 227–23) in France, for example, forbids fixing, recording, or transmitting the pornographic image of a minor and the distribution of that image. On 20 November 1996, on a day declared *National Day of Child Rights*, the French Government tightened up laws relating to the protection of the rights of the child. Among other things, then Prime Minister Alain Juppé, Justice Minister Jacques Toubon and Secretary of State for Humanitarian Relief and Action Xavier Emmanuelli announced measures making 'virtual images' sent over the Internet also subject to laws governing pornography, and criminalised the possession of pornography as well as production and distribution. None of the Eastern European countries just a short train ride away from Paris, on the other hand, has laws directed at child pornography. In May 1997, following a meeting in Buenos Aires, Interpol's Standing Group for Offences against Minors called upon police forces world-wide to infiltrate paedophile networks and maintain surveillance of the Internet, and upon governments to cooperate in dismantling pornography networks.[22] Most commentators, however, believe that the answer might lie in the hands of the service providers, who alone have the technology and know-how to effectively regulate what is happening on the Internet. There are therefore loud calls for self-regulation within the industry.

In late December 1995 and early January 1996, four million subscribers to CompuServe, one of the world's biggest Internet service providers, were denied access to 200 Internet newsgroups following complaints from German authorities that CompuServe was facilitating access to pornographic materials. Civil rights advocates complained bitterly against what they saw as an attack on freedom of speech. Amongst the newsgroups blocked by CompuServe were forums on gay and lesbian issues, homosexuality and AIDS and sex education. 'Each of the newsgroups that was suspended was specifically identified to CompuServe by the German authorities as illegal under German criminal law,' the company said.[23] Manfred Warwick, Munich's senior public prosecutor, denied that such a list was provided. The episode seemed very much to be a case of concern followed by overreaction. Interestingly, however, this case did illustrate some important issues surrounding access to pornographic materials via the Internet. First, CompuServe's German spokesman, Arno Edelmann, complained that the investigators who searched the company's offices had 'scant knowledge of computer technology and how the on-line world works' – a clear indication of the importance of involving computer industry professionals themselves in the discussion and action against sexual exploitation of children via the Internet. Second, German authorities were prompted to review existing laws criminalising child pornography and to begin review of their effectiveness. Third, CompuServe set an intelligent example to other service providers when, after the initial overreaction to threats of legal action, it fine-tuned its blocking policy and eventually lifted the restriction on access to newsgroups to just five forums specifically linked to paedophilia.[24] Moreover, CompuServe made available to its users a software programme called 'Cyber

Patrol', which allows individual computer users (or their parents) to restrict access to materials on the Internet in conjunction with CompuServe's new 'Parental Controls Centre'.[25]

Other cases similar to the CompuServe case in Germany followed, and it is obvious that the debate on Internet access and the need to protect children from abuse of it is going to continue. In May 1996, two of France's biggest service providers, WorldNet and FranceNet, were also called to task by authorities for their role in transmitting paedophile information via the Internet. Again, the materials were being exchanged anonymously through newsgroups. 'WorldNet distributes 6900 newsgroups every day, and we receive between 50 000 and 100 000 contributions [to the discussions] from the whole world daily through France Telecom,' Xavier Niel, director of WorldNet, was quoted as saying.[26] The implication was that the task of screening all this material is too huge for a service provider with only 50 staff to be able to do cost-effectively. Instead, Mr Niel believes, there should be a 'clean-up committee' common to all service-providers, a sort of 'clearing house' of messages. Such a 'censorship group' might also worry freedom of speech advocates.

Importantly, Xavier Niel based his 'not our responsibility' argument on the fact that WorldNet is only a means of transport, not a distributor or producer, and that it is therefore not responsible for the content of the messages it transports. Similar cases, with similar arguments about ultimate responsibility and freedom of speech, surfaced in the United States, Denmark, Belgium, Australia and Singapore in 1996. In December 1996, in a new move against Internet transmission of pornography, the Swiss arm of the organisation Defence for Children International brought a civil case against Internet Prolink, a Geneva-based Internet service-provider, citing Penal Code articles relating to incitement to prostitution and providing pornography to children. Prolink argued strongly that it had no way to control the images it provided 'transport' for.[27]

Meanwhile, the fight against more traditional forms of child pornography resulted in some spectacular successes by mid-1997. Most publicised was the case of 'Toro Bravo', an international pornography business run out of Colombia by a group of French porn-makers and traffickers including Jean-Manuel Vuillaume and Michel Caignet. By the time of their trial in June 1997, records and cassettes seized in the course of the investigation had led to some 600 people in France being called in for questioning by French police. More than 300 cassettes and 440 documents containing child pornography had been seized and led to more names and wider investigations. Despite these important breakthroughs in the battle against exploitation of children through pornography, however, little has yet been done to fight such exploitation on the Internet. The time has obviously come to make some international decisions on how to protect children from abuse of the superhighway.

Computers, even when they are not connected to the Internet, advance so rapidly that they continue to give law-makers and child rights workers headaches. Whereas once, for example, producers of child pornography were limited by the low technology of the still camera, computers are so versatile that they allow today's porn merchants to generate child pornography even without using a child. It is a fairly simple operation on the latest generation of computers to visually paste the head of a child on to the body of an adult woman, to reduce the size of the breasts, remove pubic hair and so give the impression that it is a child engaged in sexual acts. Although many freedom of speech activists argue that this is not therefore child pornography because it does not involve a child's body, it may still be used to coerce children to provide sex or pose for pornography, and it still sends out the 'child sex is fine' message that reassures abusers and confuses children.

Beyond the collage method of manufacturing child pornography, new technologies suggest that soon porn-producers will be able to construct pornographic sex scenes using virtual, created images of children, so that there is no real child involved at all. Not only might this by-pass many existing pornography laws based on harm done to an 'actual child', it also raises questions relating to how you define a 'virtual child'. For example, how do you decide the 'child's' age?

As Ron O'Grady has warned, 'Computer technology is still in its infancy. What the next generation of development will bring is probably taking shape in a garage near you.'[28]

This picture of a child pornography cottage industry takes many people by surprise. With talk of global transmission networks, film production set-ups and high technology, it might be supposed that child pornography is big business. It can be profitable, but in general large crime syndicates are not so active in this field as small home-based industries are. Almost all child pornography is the work of amateurs or semi-professionals filming in the homes of exploiters. Many of the producers are exploiters themselves and often appear in the films.

Their job has been made easier by advances in home video technology. Where once child porn merchants would have had to take films to be developed, and risk being found out, they are now protected by the arrival of videotape, which records a digital image and does not have to be developed. Domestic video cameras – camcorders – are simple to use, inexpensive and produce high-quality images. Once the production is complete, it can be shown on home video playback machines, VCRs, which can also be used to produce multiple copies of the tape for distribution amongst like-minded friends, or as a 'passport' to paedophile networks, including those which operate through the Internet. In November 1996, British newspapers singled out the computer skills of a Roman Catholic priest, Father Adrian McLeish, in stories detailing his conviction for sexual abuse of young boys.

'Father Adrian McLeish, *The Guardian* reported,[29] 'used his computer skills to build the biggest collection of child pornography discovered. The material, on four computers and including 9000 images, would have filled the 24-volume *Encyclopaedia Britannica* 11 times over.' McLeish made contact with young boys through their families' links to the church and groomed them to take part in sexual acts. Not content with abusing the children, McLeish boasted about it in e-mail messages and paedophile chat networks on the Internet. Police investigations in the United States into paedophile contacts via the Internet had led to the identification of 37 men who were exchanging pornographic images – some, according to reports, of children as young as two years of age - and the trail eventually led to McLeish. The case was the first in the United Kingdom where a link was proven between exchange of pornographic messages and sexual exploitation of children. The children, said the judge who sentenced McLeish to six years in jail, looked up to him and trusted him. When police spoke to them after McLeish's arrest, they were found to be suffering 'mood swings ... asthma, eczema, migraine and night-mares, and [to] have become sad, uncommunicative and fearful'.

Advances in computer and multimedia technology, then, which open up so many new opportunities for improving the life of children, can also con-tribute to their sexual exploitation. Poverty, desperation, the opening up of borders which makes trafficking of children easier, rampant consumerism, inequalities in economic distribution, confusing media images, twisted values and misplaced morals, war and displacement, religion and cultural values: a long list of factors which can make children vulnerable.

Vulnerability in this sense defines the 'supply' side of the market. As a result of the factors discussed here, often working in combination, children may be transformed into product, a worldwide 'stock' of chattels trapped in a series of frightening equations that reads:

Supply: $\quad s + e = se \quad = \quad$ vulnerable child
Demand: $\quad se + x = sex \quad = \quad$ sexual exploitation

Where s is the child, e is the factor or factors that make that child vulnerable to exploitation, and x represents the perverts who exploit children for their own sexual ends.

4 Who wants to sleep with a ten-year-old? The demand side of the equation

Monsters do not get close to children; nice men do. A chilling thought, but an important truth that comes from the experience of Ray Wyre, of Britain's Lucy Faithful Foundation, who has worked with paedophiles for many years. Father Shay Cullen, of the Preda Foundation, which works against sexual exploitation of children in the Philippines, confirms Ray Wyre's assessment. 'If you were to talk to a paedophile on the streets and have a beer with him,' Father Cullen says, 'this would be the nicest and friendliest and most charming of people you could meet. They are not beasts and monsters. They are so nice and so good and so generous that they win the trust of children. This whole masquerade of deception is a very hateful and evil thing.'[1]

It is most shocking, frustrating and frightening to those whose children fall prey to sex exploiters and abusers, that they did not recognise the person as a predator. At times it seems people expect sex exploiters to have horns, or a forked tail. But the reality is that they do not stand out in a crowd, they are not recognisably different. In fact, although we might hesitate at using the word, they usually seem absolutely 'normal'.

Sexual predators, however, are not one homogenous group. They fall into a number of different categories which we are studying and learning more about, with a view to finding ways to stop them committing their perverted crimes.

Paedophiles – from thought to deed

The group that gets most of the headlines, perhaps because of the compact neatness and universal recognition of the name given to them, is the people who are called 'paedophiles'. Paedophilia is a clinical condition which refers to an adult 'who has a personality disorder which involves a specific and focused sexual interest in prepubertal children'.[2] Most paedophiles are men, although there are also some women in the ranks and, although some of them have a preference for either boys or girls, some have no such preference.

Among paedophiles, there are some who never go beyond sexual fantasising about very young children, although the fact that some of them use child pornography as an aid to these fantasies does implicate them in exploitation.

Some, however, act upon their impulses and abuse children either in a 'non-contact' way, by exposing their genitals, showing children pornographic images and generally 'talking smutty' to children, or in a 'contact' form, touching and fondling the children, or attempting or forcing sexual penetration.

Many paedophiles identify closely with their child victims, showing to the outside world an emotional attachment to the child that can fool people into considering that the paedophile is a 'kind uncle', a generous friend of the family, someone who wishes no harm. Researchers believe that such men identify in some way with the child's vulnerability, and themselves have a sense of weakness that gives them empathy with the child. Such men often shower the children with gifts, or help pay for their education, or otherwise ingratiate themselves. Gradually this puts them in a position where they no longer feel weak like the child, but can dominate and experience the feeling of power over a weaker human being, and this can give them the opportunity they seek to move to act.

Paedophiles are also blind to the nature of their exploitation. They convince themselves that the child will not be harmed by sexual relations with an adult. They tell themselves that the child is lucky to be learning about sex from someone who cares so much and that they are therefore doing the child a service. Gerald Hannon, who claims he is not a paedophile but merely a male prostitute who advocates on behalf of paedophiles, repeats all these arguments ad infinitum.

'It makes good educational sense', Hannon wrote in 1994, 'to push a child's limits, much as we do in sports or academics, by requiring of them things they might at first feel incapable of doing ... We introduce children to many pleasurable things in life. There's no *a priori* reason why we shouldn't introduce them to sex. We don't expect kids to teach each other the violin or take themselves to church, so why do we leave kids to discover sex alone and in the dark, with no guide but their peers?'

This is a particularly odious argument when you consider that Gerald Hannon is also a teacher. When Hannon's advocacy stance on paedophilia became known, and his face was recognised in child pornography, the Canadian university where he taught suspended him. He argued that he had spoken only obliquely about child sex, and was protected in any case by the doctrine of academic freedom. Child rights activists saw matters differently. 'I don't think paedophilia is an academic subject,' Judy Steed, a writer on sexual abuse said, 'just as racist hate speech is banned in Canada, there should be no protection for advocacy of sex with children.'[3]

Hannon persists. He hates child abuse as much as anyone else does, he says, and he would never abuse a child. It is just that children *want* sex at an early age. They deserve to experience sex from someone older, who cares for them and can introduce them to sex 'without coercion and fear'. He cites examples of men he knows who had under-age sexual experiences and remember them fondly. He has a repertoire of stories that justify his stand.

But Judy Steed has a wider repertoire of case studies. She has talked extensively to boys who learned about sex from what Hannon calls 'boy-lovers'. She has seen their broken lives, their alcohol and drug abuse. She has documented the students who dropped out of college, the children who turned to crime. 'You are confronted with an avalanche of despair,' she writes. 'When Hannon advocates for adults having sex with children, and says how delightful it can be, what he doesn't do is tell the other side of the story.' Steed believes that Hannon's claim that not all children's lives are damaged by sex is tantamount to a reporter leaving Belsen convinced that some Jews found it just fine. 'And even if children did, in some unknowing, physical way, enjoy it,' she continues, 'it would be irrelevant. You can do anything you want to a child. You can have sex with a child, you can feed a child heroin. The drug will taste good and the child won't know about the future damage it's going to cause. What Hannon cannot remember – or chooses to forget - is that as children we are so dependent. Children are not little adults and, if you impose adult sexual needs on a child, you destroy that person's right to develop their own sexuality.'

The most damning condemnation of Hannon's campaign on behalf of paedophiles, however, comes not from scientific research but from his own telephone answering machine. According to news reports, an adult man called every day for three months, sometimes 40 times a day. The man talks in child whispers, 'Daddy, you hurt my bum-bum. I'm going to tell mummy. Oh Daddy, poo-poo with blood came out. I love you Daddy...' This continues until the man can no longer go on and breaks down. Hannon claims it is a crank caller. It is more likely a victim of exploitation. The call was traced to a leading Toronto law firm.[4]

None of Hannon's claims come as a surprise to those who work with paedophiles and sex offenders. So predictable are the arguments, in fact, that psychiatrists can predict what offenders will say. Drawing upon this repetitive experience, psychiatrists have been able to work with police in sexual abuse cases and have had some remarkable successes.

The two British men who were sentenced to life imprisonment for the murder of nine-year-old Daniel Handley in May 1996 were caught with the cooperation of a psychiatrist who had met them and who matched their profiles to the Handley murder case.

Timothy Moss, 33, and Brett Tyler, 30, had told the psychiatrist about their paedophile fantasies long before they moved from thought to deed. Moss, in particular, had said that he fantasised about kidnapping and murdering a young blond, blue-eyed boy. Daniel Handley fulfilled that fantasy. He was abducted in London in October 1994, sexually abused and then strangled. His body was found in April 1995 on a golf course in Bristol, in the west of England.

Moss pleaded guilty to the murder of Daniel Handley; Tyler admitted only to the kidnapping. Some paedophiles do work alone, some with partners. Quite often, however, paedophiles like to share their experiences, pornography and even their victims with others. They seek out others who will accept their desperate need to justify, rationalise and approve the acts they commit on children. Sometimes, this group of sympathisers will exchange letters (a very common paedophile trait which has now graduated, too, to the e-mail services of the Internet), share pornography and meet from time to time in an intimate 'club', small-time and secretive. In this compulsive desire to share information and record their 'conquests', paedophiles also keep diaries and detailed information about the children they exploit:

> The occupant of the apartment was an expatriate. Since he had come to Pagsanjan [Philippines] in 1981, he seemed to have kept meticulous records of local children. Some children had up to ten 3 × 5 index cards, each one neatly typed backgrounds on each child, with ages, address, body shape, what type of sex was obtained from the child. On the back of each card was the amount of money paid to each child, and other information concerning genital size, circumcised or not.[5]

The expatriate in question here was arrested and the materials found in his apartment used in evidence against him. These records also illustrate the extent of the damage active paedophiles can wreak. When police entered the home of Australian paedophile Clarence Osborne after his death, they found detailed records of 2500 boys he had exploited during his 'career'. A survey in the United States of 403 child molesters produced even more staggering statistics: altogether these 403 men had exploited 67 000 children.[6]

Other paedophiles seek out more structured, organised networks, which can link into international rings communicating and cooperating across the globe. In April 1996, 1500 people were questioned in France about suspected paedophile behaviour, in the biggest crackdown on a paedophile ring to date. Charges against some of these individuals ranged from possession of pornography to inciting minors into debauchery. A French child pornography ring reportedly copied tapes coming from Bogota, Colombia, and then forwarded them to the United States and throughout Europe. As Julia O'Connell Davidson points out,[7] the commercial profits to be made in such rings, even if they cross continents, are comparatively small, but the members satisfy their need to 'normalise' their behaviour by contact with others like themselves, gain gratification from the clandestine and risky nature of the organisation, and potentially make enough money from exchange of information and pornography, if they choose to, to finance sex tours abroad.

Not all paedophiles or sex exploiters are secretive about their preferences. Some shout it from the rooftops. Some make money from telling the world about it. These men are known as the 'intellectual paedophiles' and, just like the ordinary garden variety, they seek to rationalise their sexual exploitation of children with claims of emotional attachment, early learning experiences and caring environments. The excuses are exactly the same, only the context is different.

Hiding behind history

The so-called intellectual paedophiles have carved a niche for themselves on the bookshelves of the educated reader and, horrified at the thought that their elitist form of exploitation might be compared to the vulgar, common activity of other paedophiles, they position themselves in a long tradition of child sex exploiters which they trace back to the Ancient World. They claim that modern society refuses to acknowledge that the Ancient Greeks institutionalised what they call Man–Boy–Love (it could also be Man–Girl–Love, depending on the preference), sanctioning public displays of physical affection between men and boys in saunas and gymnasiums. They quote the Roman Emperor Tiberius (as if he were a role model to be admired!) who played 'filthy games' with children while in exile on the island of Capri; they point to ancient rituals in Papua New Guinea where the young boys fellate the elders as an initiation to manhood. They romanticise the stories of seventeenth-century French writer La Rochefoucauld and his 13-year-old girl-child love object. They inappropriately quote Wilde, Gide, Proust, Casanova, Dostoevsky ... the list of establishment literary figures they claim to 'descend' from seems endless.

These names, though, are all the names of adult men. It is much rarer to learn about the children involved in these supposedly 'mutually satisfying' relationships. Where is their voice? What do they have to say about the 'enlightenment' they are supposed to have received from these great men? Do we even know their names? Have they been elevated to the status of literary lovers like the adult women whose names we do know, like Cassandra, or Laura? No, like exploited children the world over, like the two million nameless victims of sexual exploitation hidden in the columns of statistics, these children have no identity beyond a first-name-only mention in a personal diary or a romanticised passage of imagery in a poem. To the narcissistic paedophiles who have exploited them, they are nobody.

French paedophile author Gabriel Matzneff admits that he has paid children for sex on trips to the Philippines, but rarely says how much. He has certainly made money from the books in which he describes his 'intellectual passions'. These he describes as somehow above the experience of normal mortals, a refinement of art and intellect and passion that only he and his ilk can truly appreciate. And yet the details he enters into with such relish are absolutely identical to the details that abound in investigations of child sex abuse, sex tourist convictions and sex offenders' statements: the freshness of the child and the youthful cavorting of the exploiter, the unique passion offered as a gift from a caring adult to a willing child, the student/teacher physical relationship that indicates a sense of responsibility towards the victim, the undying love that nevertheless fizzles out. Matzneff even blindly details the repercussions on the children he exploits – without seeming to acknowledge or admit any cause and effect between these symptoms and his actions:

> Vanessa is suffering, coughs her guts out, has a fever. Tired, pale, she has sudden attacks of arrythmia. Most importantly, perhaps, her mother does not seem to be aware of this weakness, this fragility ... I can say nothing to this mother who, for a year, has succeeded in the great task of accepting the central, immense, decisive place that I occupy in the heart, thoughts and daily life of her young daughter...[8]

Even when the harm he is causing his 'schoolgirl-lovers' is pointed out to him, he admits no fault but puts the blame elsewhere:

> My conversation with the mother of Marie-Elisabeth. According to her, this love, when she was an adolescent, with a man like me disturbed her very much. It was not my love for Marie-Elisabeth that disturbed her, dear lady, but the fact that I left her, eight years later. Yet again, mother got it wrong.[9]

Even as he aspires to classical elitism and lists ad nauseam the refined quality of life he leads, and the friends he has in high places, Matzneff trots out the same tired excuses that come from truck drivers, retired military men, unemployed labourers, miners, restaurateurs, drug pushers – the whole seedy gamut, in fact, of low-life paedophile men who without exception believe that they are different, that their 'love' for children is harmless, even beneficial to the child, that the child would be worse off without them. 'Vanessa', Matzneff writes in a 1986 diary account of his sexual relationship with this 14-year-old girl, 'is doing an apprenticeship, and a gentle one, since I am a faithful, irreproachable lover who gives her no real reason to suffer.'[10] Matzneff, who considers himself so different from the commonplace, so unique and special that he forms an adjective out of his name – matznevian – revels in his books in what are in fact commonplace, predictable, almost inevitable facets of paedophile behaviour, from the self-justification on the grounds of 'true love and affection', to the deception played out with unsympathetic adults, police and authorities, to the narcissistic vaunting of self (his daily weigh-ins, the endless lists of what he eats and drinks, the frequency of his manicures), to the detailed documenting of his conquests. This champion of intellectual paedophilia is, in every way except perhaps his knowledge of the classics, exactly the same as the paedophile bricklayers, truck drivers and indiscriminate retired servicemen who also think they are special and different.

Is there really, after all, any difference between making money from selling pornographic images of a child tied to a bed in a Filipino brothel, and receiving royalties for a book describing paedophile relations with an Asian child?[11] 'I would convince myself that I was different from the paedophiles I read about in the papers, and I would make people see me as X, the nice man.' X could be one of these intellectual paedophiles whose exploits appear in print; his methods and his reasoning are the same. 'You have to be an accomplished liar; that goes with the territory. Some of these people found out in the most horrific way when I abused their children that I was not quite what they thought.' In fact, X is a convicted child abuser, now in treatment to prevent him from offending again.

Controlling the urge

'Chemical castration' is the brutal way some commentators describe the drug therapy that is available in several countries to paedophiles who want help to suppress the urge to act upon their sexual fantasies. In the US state of California, it was written into a new law signed in September 1996, aimed at preventing convicted sex offenders from abusing again, and it was also one of a number of initiatives announced by the French Government in November 1996:

> The first section of the law proposes the introduction of a complementary punishment consisting of medico-social follow-up for sex offenders. The convicted person may be obliged to undergo surveillance and assistance, comprising in particular medical intervention, but only after a medical expert has indicated that the convicted person is an appropriate recipient of such treatment.[12]

According to official California statistics, more than 50 per cent of sex offenders offend again in the year following their release; 75 per cent are likely to offend again within two years. In the light of these statistics, and following the example of Sweden, Denmark and Germany, where repeat offence rates are as low as 2.2 per cent after chemical castration, California signed into law drug treatment for paedophiles on second conviction of crimes against a child below 13 years of age.

The California treatment consists of the drug DepoProvera, which reduces levels of testosterone, the male hormone, and so suppresses sexual desire. It is administered weekly after the offender is released from prison, on the advice of a judicial commission. A sentencing judge may also order drug therapy on first offence. As more experience of such medico-therapeutic treatment is gained, governments are also looking at beginning treatment while the offender is still in prison.

What is important, according to Ray Wyre, is stopping paedophiles from making the transition from fantasy to action. 'You cannot cure them,' Wyre says, 'but you can treat them and help them to control the urge to act.'

Despite the violence of its popular name, then, chemical castration is a comparatively gentle way of reducing sexual urge in a climate where, following increasingly frequent and numerous reports of children being sexually exploited, abused and killed, many people have called for much harsher penalties against offenders. No government has yet introduced harsher physical punishment – although there have been newspaper reports that some Asian governments have discussed making the death penalty mandatory for some cases of sexual exploitation of children – but many governments are now introducing packages of measures, judicial and supervisory, to try and stop offenders from abusing again.

Former British Home Secretary Michael Howard in June 1996 introduced a 'package of powers' aimed at the 1800 or so rapists, paedophiles and abusers who commit sex crimes each year in Great Britain. The measures, which came into force in January 1997, aim not to 'cure' but to 'control' and are designed to keep offenders away from situations where they might offend again, as well as alerting those responsible for children to the potential for exploitation. They include, for example, powers to ban convicted offenders from finding work which brings them into contact with children, whether that work be paid or voluntary, and to impose conditions on release, such as confining offenders to house arrest at times when children are travelling to and from school, or banning them completely from public places where children gather. As part of the intention to track convicted sex offenders, too, the British package proposes that they be required to notify the police of their address and any subsequent moves.

X, the convicted offender so lucid about the methods of paedophile exploiters, is sceptical about such measures. 'Paedophiles will find a way to beat the system,' he assured a reporter.[13] 'These people are clever and organised, so they will find a way round any regulation. They change their names or go abroad.' Even prison, X argues, is less a punishment than a way to meet other paedophiles. 'A lot of knowledge goes through those gates. There were people in jail who had been abusing for 30 or 40 years. In prison, you have a lot of like-minded people strolling about together, talking about how they can indulge their fantasies.'

John David Stamford is an excellent example of the intellectual exploiter, the classic paedophile organiser and group member, and the cunning abuser the law never quite caught up with.

On 23 November 1994, this Scottish ex-Anglican priest, 55, appeared before the tribunal of Turnhout, in Belgium.[14] He gave his name and his profession: journalist, writer and masseur. Stamford was best known, however, as editor of the *Spartacus Guide*, a publication started in 1970, whose annual updated edition sold 50 000 copies. The *Guide* came out of Berlin but was compiled in Stamford's offices in London and Amsterdam. The research for the book was done in the brothels and on the street corners of more than 150 countries where children can be bought for sex.

Stamford claimed that the *Spartacus Guide* was no more than a holiday guide catering to the needs of homosexual travellers. If it had been, no one would have considered it any more inappropriate than a tour guide for people interested in gourmet foods, interesting churches or good surf. The *Guide* was in fact a thinly veiled aid to those who wished to sexually exploit children.

Stamford was careful, however, never to explicitly publish this and, indeed, later versions of the *Guide* carried a disclaimer suggesting that child exploitation was abominable. No-one who read the text, however, could be left in any doubt about its true content:

> Spartacus has a number of boys, in Manila and the provinces, who are happy to meet tourists ... Each introduction costs six dollars or the equivalent in other currencies. Write to us and tell us the name of the boy you wish to meet, tell us your arrival date, flight number and the hotel where you will be staying. We shall write to the boy and ask him to contact you as soon as you arrive. Generally, the boys are available after the age of puberty or even before, and normally no-one objects ... You go into the hall of the hotel with your boy, take your key and go straight up to your room...

The *Spartacus Guide*, moreover, was a passport to the Spartacus Club, boasting up to 30 000 members worldwide who received 'order forms' on which they specified their requirements before travelling to meet the boys the *Guide* offered.[15] Stamford claimed to have 'tested' many of the boys himself before allowing their inclusion on the forms. 'I have personally tested many of these boys. They are well taught and give sex and massages very professionally. The prices are higher than the boys on the streets, but you might prefer this service rather than choosing boys at random.' The text continues with key words in other languages so that readers who take up the offer will know how to specify the 'service' they require and lists addresses of hotels which turn a blind eye to illegal behaviour.

In 1987, Stamford was arrested in the Netherlands. He was released on freedom of speech technicalities. In 1992, he was arrested in Germany and was released on the grounds that there was not sufficient evidence to convict him, despite a journalist's testimony about a Spartacus network he had managed to infiltrate in the Philippines. In 1994, Stamford came before Belgian justice, charged with 'indecent publication' and encouraging sexual exploitation of children by adults, offences carrying a maximum jail sentence of one year. Child rights activists joined in a campaign to have the charges changed to 'facilitating, aiding and encouraging paedophiles to corrupt children' and to trafficking. Under these articles of the Belgian Penal Code, Stamford faced up to 20 years in jail.

Moreover, the child rights organisations had worked to ensure that this time Stamford would not get off because the evidence did not seem conclusive. François Lefort, a French priest working to rescue children from sex on the streets, had arranged a clandestine meeting with Stamford, posing as a rich paedophile looking for 'young flesh'. He met Stamford in a dirty movie house in Amsterdam. Lefort's testimony was that Stamford's response was clear, 'For US$500 [£300], I am the only person who can provide to you, within two hours, a child of either sex anywhere in the world.'

This time, it seemed, child rights workers would win their battle on behalf of sexually exploited children. But fate intervened: John Stamford died on 27 December 1995, of natural causes, before his case could be brought to a conclusion.

A long overseas tour

Child rights activists also worked hard in the cases of Michael Clarke and Victor Fitzgerald. Michael Clarke, 49, was arrested in Olangapo City, Philippines, on 5 June 1995. The British expatriate was charged under Article III, Section 5, Paragraph (a), Sub-paragraphs 1 and 2 of the Republic Act 7610, which reads, 'The penalty of *reclusion temporal* in its medium period to *reclusion perpetua* shall be imposed upon the following: 1. Acting as a procurer of a child prostitute and 2. Inducing a person to be a client of a child prostitute by means of written or oral advertisement or other similar means.' The complainants were listed as Father Shay Cullen and Rolanda Besarra, Executive Director and Paralegal Officer.

Shay Cullen is better known as 'that Irish priest'. He has been the scourge of Olangapo City since the early seventies, when he decided someone had to do something about the commercial sexual exploitation of children in this Philippine city once home to the GIs from Subic Bay. Shay Cullen deals with both sides of the equation. As Executive Director of the Preda Association, he helps vulnerable children to find ways to avoid the trap of prostitution, escape from it if they are caught and build new lives afterwards. He is positive but at the same time sceptical about the results of such work with children who have been overwhelmingly damaged by the exploitation they have suffered. Father Cullen also targets the exploiters. He follows them, documents their crimes, knows the loopholes through which they try to escape and blocks them. In 1995, he helped two British child rights agencies, Christian Aid and the Jubilee Campaign, and Adam Holloway, a reporter from London's Independent Television News (ITN), to investigate the dealings of Michael Clarke as part of a campaign to influence British members of parliament who were considering legislation against child sex tourism.

In February 1995, Jubilee began compiling information, and discussing with ITN a number of British paedophiles and sex tour operators working out of the Philippines. In March 1995, Christian Aid joined the team. Martin Cottingham, a Christian Aid officer based in London, picked up a copy of the *Exchange and Mart* newspaper and saw an ad for a tour operator named Paradise Express. He requested a brochure and received one soon after. Paradise Express was very obviously in the business of sex tourism:

> ...the best Sunday lunch in town 'The Dirty Dozen Feast' (strictly members only) for £13, *it offered,* fully inclusive of a superb lunch, as much drink as you can handle between 12 noon and 4 pm. Included in the price is a very special extra!! Choose any one of his delightful ladies for an hour's private relaxation! (Need we say more?) All John's Ladies are very understanding and will stop at nothing to please you!
>
> The Ultimate Mission £59 ... the OK Corral, where dozens of headstrong young fillies are tethered! At 10 pm you chose [*sic*] your mount, returning to the beach for an all night super bash (booze and food on tap!) The following morning you return your filly and head back to Angeles for yet another day in Paradise. In case you feel the need for a 'lay' down, our private beach cabin is freely available.

On 6 April 1995, Cottingham telephoned Michael Clarke, self-styled 'Dr Crazy' in the brochure, and recorded their conversation. When he asked whether younger girls were 'safer in the Philippines because of the threat of AIDS', Clarke asked him to call him later at home. Cottingham did, and recorded Clarke as he assured him that 'they are supposed to be around 18 to work but there are girls who are younger than that'. On 8 April, Clarke told Cottingham over the phone that he could provide 'a nice cherry girl, only been fucked a couple of times'. A few days later, on 11 April, Cottingham received more explicit publicity materials from Clarke. He called Clarke from the offices of ITN and Clarke assured him again that he could supply under-age girls. Cottingham 'booked' a tour for himself and a 'friend', ITN reporter Adam Holloway.

The pair visited Clarke's Eastbourne, England, tour office on 24 April and finalised their holiday. Clarke handed Cottingham a handwritten note confirming that the girls he had promised – including a 12-year-old – would be waiting. He told Cottingham 'it's OK to open them up front and back' as long as violence is not used 'as this may lead to police involvement'.

Cottingham and Holloway packed their bags and left on 29 April. On arrival in the Philippines, they contacted Preda. There they learned about the rules of cooperation, socio-legal implications of their investigation, responsibilities relating to the child victims, offenders, pimps and traffickers. Armed with this understanding, Cottingham and the reporter set off on 2 May for Angeles City and the 'ultimate Adult Disney World' Clarke had promised. They checked in at a hotel specified in Michael Clarke's instructions, and met Clarke himself. Unaware of the hidden camera they had with them, he offered them 12-year-old girls and then left for Olangapo City 'on a fishing trip'.

On 5 May, Cottingham received a fax from Clarke asking them to come to Olangapo, where children would be waiting for them on the beach. On 7 May, an ITN film crew arrived at the designated beach, and met Michael Clarke. On camera he denied offering children for sex.

The film was shown on CNN's *Inside Asia* report on 16 May and seen by Senator Ernesto Herrera of the Philippines Government. On 5 June, Herrera contacted Preda and asked for help in locating Clarke. Two hours later, agents of the National Bureau of Investigation arrested Clarke and, on 6 June, he was detained without bail.

On 16 October, Cottingham and Clarke met again, this time across a courtroom where Clarke threatened Cottingham as he gave evidence. 'He told me I was dead meat, threatening to send his brother to my home with a baseball bat.'[16] The next day, Father Shay Cullen presented as evidence in court the brochures Cottingham had received, photographs of a poster advertising Clarke's tours, the fax sent to Cottingham's hotel, a video excerpt of the ITN report and the original news clipping from the *Exchange and Mart* that had started the investigation. In his testimony, Cullen expressed outrage at a picture he had seen on the wall of the house where Clarke was staying, advertising a beach party and depicting a young Filipino boy 'naked which was obscene to us as it appeared to show the child's erect sexual organ. The child was tied, gagged and being roasted on a spit.'

Cottingham detailed to the court the chronology of his dealings with Clarke and, on 10 January 1996, the prosecution rested its case. On 11 October 1996, Michael Clarke was sentenced to 16 years in a Philippine jail followed by deportation.[17]

Clarke was an obvious success story. Many more cases have been brought to trial and failed on technicalities, or because the children's families have been bought to restrain the child from testifying – hence the importance of crusaders like Shay Cullen themselves being able to obtain and give evidence. In the past, too, many foreign men have skipped bail, obtained a replacement passport and returned home before their case came to court, although that is becoming more difficult with the widespread introduction of extraterritoriality legislation, which allows their own police to pursue them for crimes committed overseas, and raise awareness of the criminal nature of sexual exploitation of children among overseas diplomatic mission staff.

Increasingly, commercial sexual exploiters of children are being brought to justice and sent to prison: Bradley Pendragon, Australian, 2.5 years in Thailand; Steven Mitchell, British, 17 years in the Philippines; John Mayland, Australian, 8.5 years in Australia; Marcio Luix de Carvalho, Brazilian, 6 years in Brazil; Bengt Bohlin, Swede, 3 months and a fine, in Thailand; Dennis Jones, British Guyanan, 40 years in Thailand; Michel Dikranian, French, 20 years in France; Gavin Scott, British, 2 years in Cambodia. The list goes on and includes Italians, Germans, Dutch, Swiss, Americans. The cases which are coming to court are increasing and the sentences are becoming harsher as governments all over the world, in the 'sending' as well as the 'receiving' countries of sex tourists, are cracking down on people who exploit children for sex.

Victor Fitzgerald, a 66-year-old retired Australian furniture removalist, was finally convicted in 1996 after a three-year battle to put him behind bars.[18] Fitzgerald sailed his rebuilt timber trimaran from Darwin, Australia, to the Philippines in 1992, and made the tactical error of anchoring off the coast near Preda's headquarters in Olangapo City. Shay Cullen became suspicious when he saw children playing on the boat, and asked federal police to investigate. Preliminary investigations failed to show conclusive wrongdoing, although Fitzgerald was on board the boat alone with three young children, including a 13-year-old named Gloria.

A few months later, Cullen tried again and this time urged Gloria and her friend, Jacqueline, to file rape and child-abuse charges. The cases came to trial before separate judges. Fitzgerald was acquitted of offences against Jacqueline when Gloria testified that Fitzgerald had not sexually assaulted them. In her own case, however, Gloria testified that Fitzgerald had fondled and attempted intercourse with her and other children on his boat. She said Fitzgerald had given them clothing and money. Fitzgerald was acquitted of rape but convicted of attempting to entice Gloria into prostitution with gifts of money and other goods. He was sentenced to between eight and 17 years in prison and was ordered to pay Gloria US$1900 (£1150) in damages.

The most confusing aspect of cases like that brought against Fitzgerald and other exploiters is that the evidence of the children sometimes seems contradictory. This is not surprising, though, when you consider the pressures the child is under. Gloria, the judge considered in this case, 'was under intense pressure not to divulge the sexual abuses she encountered', not only from Fitzgerald, but her family, friends and a society that stigmatises children who have been victims of sexual offences. Her mother and uncle, she said, 'told me I will have a big amount of money if I side with Fitzgerald'. Gloria was removed from her mother's custody and made a ward of state. Charges of negligence against her mother were eventually dropped, on the basis that her negligence was probably not intentional – Gloria was the youngest of eight children and essentially just allowed to run free.

Fitzgerald, predictably, argued that he was 'convicted on the evidence [he] was acquitted on' and appealed to a higher court. His only crime, he said, was being generous to the poor people he met in the Philippines.

Shay Cullen's involvement in the case was again decisive. He alerted police to Fitzgerald's boat in the first place, and he supported Gloria and the other children throughout the case. According to Fitzgerald, 'he needed a scapegoat and he got me'. But it is difficult to see how Shay Cullen benefits in any way from the convictions of people like Clarke and Fitzgerald. He is not making a profit from his work; he continues to live in Olangapo and has not sought international fame or status. While Gloria stood to receive money (hardly to 'gain', though) whether she testified for or against Fitzgerald, and Fitzgerald had his retirement home, his lifestyle and his freedom to lose, Father Cullen worked on the Fitzgerald case for three years with no promise of 'reward' other than the knowledge that, if Fitzgerald were convicted, a few more children would be safe from sexual exploitation and potentially the message would get out to other exploiters considering following his example.

Paedophiles and child sex tourists. They come in all shapes and sizes. ECPAT analysis of the 240 foreigners who sexually abused children in Asia between 1989 and 1996 and who were arrested, imprisoned, deported or who escaped without penalty, shows how diverse these perverts are.[19]

Twenty-five per cent of the exploiters came from the United States, 16 per cent from Germany, 13 per cent from the United Kingdom, 12 per cent from Australia, 7 per cent from Japan and France; the rest came from, in descending order of statistical significance: Canada, Switzerland, Sweden, Denmark, Austria, Belgium, Netherlands, Norway, Spain, Saudi Arabia and South Africa. Most of the men (33 per cent) were aged between 40 and 50 years; 24 per cent between 50 and 60 years; 18 per cent between 30 and 40; 15 per cent between 60 and 70; 7 per cent were between 20 and 30 years of age and 3 per cent were over 70. Although most of the exploiters did not specify or hid their occupation, 15 gave their occupation as 'social or aid worker', potentially reflecting the fact that this is the profession they set themselves up in in order to obtain access to the children, the same as those who said they were 'travel agents'. Some of the men were retired but, of those still in employment, the largest group of exploiters were teachers, followed by doctors, engineers, clergy, local men and other professionals – a list that is overwhelmingly made up of men whose jobs put them in a position of trust towards children.

Heinrich Stefan Ritter is a medical doctor. This Austrian paedophile has gone down in history as the first foreigner to be convicted in the Philippines for sexual intercourse with an under-age child. But the story that is told is not his; it is the story of Rosario Baluyot, a young child not so different from thousands of others caught up in commercial sexual exploitation, but whose death caused such a public outcry that it is seen as a turning point in the campaign to make people aware of how children are sold for sex, and what can become of them. As Ron O'Grady has written, 'in a curious way [Rosario's story] seems to sum up all the defeat and humiliation of the poor who are used and abused by weak people with the power of a few dollars'.

Rosario's story

Rosario was born in Olangapo, the youngest of eight children. Her mother, Anita, had been much abused and was living with Policarpio Baluyot, her third partner, when Rosario was born. Rosario was her last child. Anita died of a brain tumour at the age of 36, leaving Policarpio with the five children she had borne him.

He sold a son to a procurer and moved the others to a cult village called Sacrifice Valley. Soon after, he found a new wife and moved to a town called Pampanga, leaving the children behind. He never contacted them again. Left in the care of a group of religious zealots, the two eldest children ran off, leaving Rosario and her young brother alone. She was only about six years old. By the time she was eight, Rosario was well known as a trouble-maker and petty thief, and made her way to Olangapo City and the American naval base at Subic Bay. There she did what so many of the street children of Olangapo did: she learned to live off the servicemen at the base. 'They have good teachers,' Ron O'Grady writes,[20] 'The town is full of people who have learned the lessons of life on the streets. An estimated 25 000 prostitutes live in Olangapo and that number doubles when a large naval vessel enters the port.'

Rosario did not live all the time on the streets. She had a room in a house owned by a woman named Violet, a Dickensian character who sent the children out to beg and pick pockets and took the money for herself. Rosario was a tough character. They called her 'tomboy' because she would win fights even with those bigger than herself. She shaved her hair off and learned to use the drugs that children of the streets use to take away the pain and memories. With little left to value except her inner dignity, Rosario seems to have found a way to survive in this rough life. Then, in 1986, Violet's common-law husband Jimmy raped her. Now Rosario had not even her dignity to hold on to, and like many others before and after, she saw no reason not to take the opportunity of earning more money by selling the body that had been devalued to men willing to pay for it.

She met first John, a paedophile retired naval officer in his fifties, who gave her US$20 (£12). Violet took most of it. John was the first of many. Twenty dollars is a lot of money for a little girl who has never had anything, and soon she accepted anyone who was willing to pay. She told her friends about an American who 'poked things into her vagina', first a lipstick tube, then the top of a shampoo bottle. Sometimes he gave her drugs and when she woke up she had no idea what had happened.

So Rosario's life took on a pattern of clients, abuse, money, no money, more clients, more abuse, more money, no money ...

The date was 10 October 1986. Rosario was with Joe, a 14-year-old street friend, when a tourist stopped to talk to them and asked them to come to his hotel room. The children presumed he was American, although Joe said later he was sure the man was German. He took them back to his hotel room and shared a bath with them. He began to fondle them and then turned his attention to Rosario alone. According to Joe, the man then began 'poking something grey like a Vick's inhaler' into Rosario's vagina. She cried out several times in pain, but Joe eventually fell asleep on the bed and heard no more. When they woke up next morning, the tourist was gone.

Rosario, though, was still in pain. She told Joe that the man 'had inserted something in her private parts and left it there' and her lower abdomen hurt. For the next few days, she tried to remove whatever it was that was stuck, until the pain became so bad that she had to go to a doctor. He told her that he would remove the thing without any charge, and asked her to wait. A friend who went with her later said Rosario was frightened that the doctor would call the police and send her to prison after he had helped her. Whatever her fear, she left with the thing still stuck inside her vagina.

Rosario began to smell. Friends thought it was funny and laughed at her, but she continued her life in pain and humiliation. Jimmy, Violet's de-facto, reappeared and, although he knew she had something inside her, he raped her again. Whatever had been in her vagina moved up into her cervix. She could hardly walk now and took the pain away by sniffing glue and taking drugs. People began to mistreat her to get her to go away, as the smell got worse. She began to sleep on the streets and on empty lots, and she grew dirty and fly-ridden.

On 14 May 1987, a neighbour was wheeling a cart when he saw a group of people on the street. They were crowded around Rosario, who writhed in pain on the floor, a green discharge coming from her mouth. The neighbour lifted her on to his cart and pushed her to hospital.

Doctors examined Rosario and found her abdomen grossly enlarged. Her pain was so bad they could hardly touch her. They gave her painkillers and, when they could finally operate, they found in her uterus a broken vibrator nine centimetres long. It had a jagged edge and a rusty screw still hanging on the side. It had been inside Rosario's body for months. Now, with the object removed, Rosario still suffered. Septicaemia had set in, and her internal organs were wasted from sniffing glue. At 2.15 pm on 19 May 1987, Rosario Baluyot died of heart failure. This child who had lived a hundred lives and died a thousand deaths was 11 or 12 years old.

Four months later, the events surrounding Rosario's death were still being discussed. A nun, Sister Eva Palencia, who had been at Rosario's side when she died, ensured that people knew what had happened and kept up pressure to find the man who had killed her. The story had made headlines and the press were speculating that the man was an American serviceman from the Subic Bay naval base. Joe, though, continued to insist that the man was German. And then an Austrian tourist in Manila admitted to police that he had been with Rosario on the night when the vibrator had been inserted. The police arrested Heinrich Stefan Ritter, a 32-year-old doctor, and charged him with the murder of Rosario. Incredibly, this man charged with murder was granted bail and negotiated an out-of-court settlement with Rosario's relatives. Social workers and public pressure at this injustice convinced the judge to reverse this decision and eventually, in a blaze of press outrage, Ritter went to trial.

Thirty witnesses gave evidence at the trial, but Joe was the most important. He identified Ritter as the man with whom they had gone back to the hotel.

On 29 March 1989, Heinrich Ritter was sentenced to life imprisonment for the rape and death of Rosario Baluyot. Two years later, he was free.

On 5 March 1991, the Supreme Court of the Philippines reversed the judgement and, in a 45-page decision, acquitted him on the grounds that Rosario was 12 years old, not 11, and that the revised Penal Code stipulated that rape is committed only if the woman is under 12 years of age. They also found reason to doubt that Ritter was, in fact, the man who had inserted the vibrator into Rosario's vagina, because she had earlier told friends that an 'American' did that to her. Another street child told police this was Tony, an American serviceman in his mid-thirties, a paedophile and drug taker. Many believe Ritter was set up to avoid trouble with the American authorities. The debate continues.

Ron O'Grady quotes[21] an editorial in the Philippines *Daily Enquirer* which succinctly sums up feelings in that country, and elsewhere, about Rosario's death:

> the case of Rosario illustrates all too graphically how the material poverty can also lead to the impoverishment of human dignity. Most people are no longer shocked that children roam our cities as street walkers. We have come to look at them as but one of the many consequences of our underdevelopment, hoping that such 'rational' analysis would give us the excuse to stop caring. But how many Rosarios will it take for us to realise that for each boy or girl who gets sucked into the sex trade, who perishes at the hands of perverts, we allow an important piece of ourselves to be destroyed as well? A society that is unable to guarantee the safety and

well-being of its most vulnerable members – the young – is a society that is on the verge of disintegration. Rosario died as she had lived. Ignored. Uncared for. Traded like any other commodity in the market. The victim of a society that has become as spiritually impoverished as it is materially poor.[22]

The name of Rosario Baluyot will not be forgotten. Now it has been joined by those of Daniel Handley, Julie Lejeune, Mélissa Russo. The day will come when the names of their killers – the men who valued sex more than children – are as well known, and are reviled.

Packs on the prowl

There is another group of men who sexually exploit children, and these are the ones Julia O'Connell Davidson calls 'the Macho Men'.

The Macho Men travel in small packs and like to think of themselves as something special. In their regular daily lives, this is not easy, because usually they are in humdrum jobs and not particularly wealthy. Once in a foreign country, however, they have spending power, suntans and like to ape what they see as the 'lifestyles of the rich and famous'. This means a better class of hotel than they would normally stay at, plenty of food and drink and an armful of young girls to flatter their egos. Although the Macho Men do not necessarily seek out under-age girls for sex, they are morally and sexually indiscriminate and rarely bother to ask the girls' ages. As the 1980s song by the rock band Dragon says, 'I wanted someone to kiss/You were standing there/So tell me the truth/Are you old enough?'

O'Connell Davidson met Macho Men Joe and Pete in the Dominican Republic.[23] They were part of a group of five miners from Yorkshire, England, who were on a sex tour. O'Connell Davidson describes Joe as 'heavily tattooed, a large Union Jack emblazoned on his upper arm' and says all five men divided their time on holiday between sunbathing, drinking free beer at the hotel and having sex with teenage Dominican girls. Unlike paedophile men who pick up children in informal sex trade settings but deny that there is any element of prostitution involved, claiming rather that the children are friends, companions or in a caring relationship, the Macho Men freely admit that the girls they are having sex with are 'prostitutes'. Much of the rest of the fantasy is the same, though. Joe and Pete, for example, illustrated clearly the desire to dominate that had characterised the paedophile interviews O'Connell Davidson conducted, as well as the wishful thinking that the girls are actually attracted to them in some way: 'This one [gestures towards the girl at his side] come down the beach with us. They rub in the sun tan oil, bring us the towel, she even washes your feet. What English tart would do that? The problem is getting rid of them. Once you've bought them, they stick to you. They even fight with each other over you. It's wicked.'

Both Joe and Pete are also reported to have pointed out how young some of the girls are, claiming that they 'wouldn't go with a girl like that'. And yet Pete was accompanied by a 17-year-old girl during the interview, and seemed only to care about how old the girl *looked*, not how old she *was*. As O'Connell Davidson concludes, 'there is no reason to suppose these men consciously and deliberately seek out under-age girls to sexually exploit. Equally, there is no reason to be confident that they have not exploited, or would not sexually exploit, a girl as young as 14 or 15 providing that she did not "look about 12".' In short, O'Connell Davidson's 'Macho Men' are what some commentators call 'men who don't give a damn'. Not only do these men buy children for sex, they do so almost 'by accident', sexually exploiting a child without a second thought. Such behaviour is morally reprehensible. What makes it even more despicable is that the men seem often to be fully aware of their immorality: 'You forget your morals here and lower your standards and allow yourself to get swept along by baser instincts. Back home there is always a reminder – the area is run-down, the girls look like sluts, the bars are seedy. Here you don't have to face any of that: the girls are childlike, the bars relaxed. Prostitution has a clean face here.'[24] Kinder commentators also call these men 'situational abusers', to reflect the fact that they do not necessarily intend to buy children for sex; it 'just happens'.

What is also reprehensible in this group of exploiters, as in others who travel to other countries specifically to buy other human beings, including children, for sex, is the thinly veiled racism they commonly manifest. These ostensibly kindly, fun-loving men, who only want to help out a poor child or spend a few hours with a young working girl, speak about the children they exploit as if they were inferior beings.

'Sex is a natural thing here. Everyone's at it. Fathers do it with their daughters; brothers do it with their sisters; they don't care. They'll do it with anyone; they don't care who it is or how old they are. They're like animals . . . They're like dogs or cats or roosters. Have you seen roosters, the way in the farmyard the way they carry on? Just hop on top of any chicken they see. That's what it's like here. By the time a girl is 10 years old, she's had more experience than, well, an American woman or an Irish woman won't never have . . . Girls learn it's the way to keep a man happy. It's natural to them. It's a natural way to please men.'

This American man on holiday in the Dominican Republic is married with two children.[25] His views of 'other cultures' are not uncommon. Desperate to find an excuse for buying children for sex, most exploiters suggest that it is somehow 'normal' in the country they are visiting, because the people there are even more morally lax than they are. While these model citizens only exploit children while they are on holiday, the foreigners they buy 'do it all the time'. In truth, of course, just about every society condemns sexual irresponsibility, especially in the under-age, and the children these men exploit are or become outcasts in their own communities. These world travellers, however, are not on holiday to immerse themselves in the culture and traditions of another race, nor to learn the language so that they can begin to understand. They are on holiday for sex and their racism helps them to rationalise this: 'It's wrong in our culture, but not for Africans,' Jim, a married South African sex tourist, told O'Connell Davidson.[26] 'African girls are all married by the time they're 14. Girls grow up very young. They're often having sex when they're 12. So can you say that's wrong when it's their tradition?' Jim's friend agreed with him and explained that 'Africans' – by which he meant Africans with black skin, not white like his – attach different meanings to sexual behaviour, which their culture sees as something 'very primitive'. To illustrate this, he explained how Zulu chiefs 'like lots of cows and big, fat women to prove they're wealthy'. O'Connell Davidson asked him whether the fact that white South African men like BMW cars and thin women to prove that they are wealthy was a sign that they, too, are 'primitive', but the point seems to have been lost on this visiting amateur anthropologist.

Among the morally indiscriminate exploiters but perhaps not specifically 'macho', are the group O'Connell Davidson has called 'beach party and surfer sex tourists'. These men are a world away from the flabby old men who exploit young boys; they are, according to O'Connell Davidson, young 'blond, bronzed, Californian surfer' types, who presumably would have no problem attracting young women of their own age and social group at home. Their reasons for travelling to Costa Rica, where O'Connell Davidson met them, and buying sex from young children, is a clear sign of the twisted values such people have. They described the scene as 'funky, party-time'. Sexual access to local people is seen as part of a 'package' that includes 'hanging out with colourful locals, gambling, dancing, drinking rum and smoking marijuana'.[27] In towns like Limon and Cahuita, girls as young as 12 have sex with these young men, but are not part of the formal prostitution sector. This helps the surfers convince themselves that they are engaged in 'colourful local' relationships, not contractual prostitution. 'It was a lot of fun,' one party animal told O'Connell Davidson about a pornographic video his friends had made the night before with some local children. 'They got up to stuff that would be illegal in the States, or even in Mexico.' In this way children's bodies are bought 'for fun' and so that privileged young men can experience 'stuff' they can boast about to their friends.

While the Macho Men, the beach party surfers and those who 'just don't give a damn' are classed by experts on the subject of child exploitation as 'situational abusers', and the paedophiles, intellectual or otherwise, who consciously choose children for sex are considered 'preferential abusers', there is one group of child sex exploiters who are regularly missing from discussions of the kinds of people who sexually exploit children.

Maternal instincts abused

These are the women who buy children for sex. Until recent times, most women paedophiles seem not to have acted upon their urges to any great extent. Potentially this was because women, even in the most affluent societies, did not have the financial and social freedom and independence to 'indulge' their fantasies to any great degree. As women have become increasingly financially independent, however, and have ventured outside the conventions of marriage and sex inside marriage, women paedophiles have also become more active.

The first signs of this seem to have been in the Caribbean, where in the 1970s wealthy women executives from the United States and Canada began to visit with the intention of buying sex from children. Generally the women would pick up young boys at the beach, although some women paid young girls to have sexual relations with them. In recent years, as the phenomenon of sex tourism has grown, women paedophiles from Western Europe are also travelling to South East Asia to exploit children.

Many of the women arriving in Asia, according to Ron O'Grady, are widows or divorcees, and the women often travel in pairs.[28] O'Grady describes the women as claiming they are 'fulfilling both [their] maternal and [their] feminine needs at once', a description which recalls to some degree the paternalistic claims of many male paedophiles. Certainly the deception of 'caring' for the children is as evident in the women who exploit children as it is in the men. It is just as false, particularly when it is considered that the women, in order to have sexual intercourse with a very young boy, inject hormones or similar drugs into the testicles of the child. This is extremely dangerous and can inflict permanent damage, causing 'a gruesome enlargement of the penis', according to a female doctor who examined children who had suffered such abuse. The same doctor considered 'that a young boy of 11 or 12 years of age could not survive more than five or six such injections'.

Despite the danger inherent in these drugs, there are reports that women travelling from Germany and Switzerland have imported them to use with child sex partners. According to O'Grady, police raids on brothels in India and Thailand have uncovered caches of sex-inducing drugs for use on both boys and girls and, in at least two cases, the drugs had been manufactured in France.

Women paedophiles do not yet seem to benefit from the support structures, clubs and networks that their male counterparts do, although this may be changing. They also rarely use the formal sex trade structures in the countries they visit: the brothels, clubs and bars. Most of their contacts are made on beaches or street corners and consequently their assignments carry more risk. There are many stories of women being robbed or assaulted while they arrange or await such assignments. It is perhaps this element of physical

danger, rather than the risk of being caught, that has made women paedophiles more cautious. There are, however, several prominent examples of
women who have sexually exploited children in their home countries,
including Rosemary West, wife of Fred West and, it seems, an equal and
aggressive partner in the sexual exploitation of young girls in England.

When police finally caught up with Rosemary West and her husband Fred
West in their Cromwell Street home which came to be known as the 'house of
horrors', there was at first public disbelief that Rosemary, a matronly, plain-
looking woman and mother, could even have known that Fred West was
abducting young girls, sexually abusing them and then murdering them and
burying them in the cellar and garden of their home. The fact that Fred West's
first wife had disappeared, presumed murdered, and that his murderous
rampage began before he even met and married Rosemary was taken by
many to indicate that Rosemary was not involved in the killings. But, they
asked, how could she not have known? How can any woman live with a man
for so many years and not be aware that he is abusing young women and
girls and then murdering them? How could Rosemary explain the disappear-
ance of a number of young women who had stayed at their home, including
one of her daughters who, she told relatives, had simply 'left home'? While
the press and the public had no difficulty whatsoever in believing that Fred
West might be a child sex abuser and murderer, the general reaction to Rosemary West was that she must have been particularly naive and stupid not to
know what was happening under her nose or that she was so dominated by
her husband that she did not dare speak out.

When Rosemary West was taken into custody, it was at first presumed that
she – like many women in the history of crime – had become an accomplice to
her husband to 'protect her man' and that this was somehow a romantic,
almost noble thing. When Fred West hanged himself in prison while awaiting trial and claimed total responsibility for the abductions, abuse and
murders, it seemed to confirm the general impression that Rosemary West
was just a woman in love, one of a string of women who had been led astray
by a man they adored.

The truth seems to have been very different. As more and more information came to light, and as young women who years before had slipped
through the Wests' clutches came forward with evidence, it became clear that
what united Fred and Rosemary West was no romantic bond; it was a web of
evil. When Fred West met Rosemary, he met his match. Witnesses told of
how Rosemary would lure them into the car that Fred was driving – young
women who might refuse a lift from a strange man felt much safer with a
woman in the car – and would fondle and abuse them herself. They told of
how she exploited them with no encouragement from Fred, how she initiated
abuse and seemed to enjoy it. And, although Fred was the one who dug the
holes and buried the girls, it was obvious too that Rosemary was more than

an accomplice in the killings not only of the strangers they had lured to the house but also of her own daughter. It was perhaps this single fact – the sexual abuse and murder of a child by her mother – that damned Rosemary West for all time in the eyes of the British public. Even Myra Hindley, the notorious 'Moors murderer' who with co-murderer Ian Brady had recorded the pleas of innocent young children as they sexually abused and then killed them, had not murdered her own child. In studies of the sexual exploitation of children, there are many times when right-thinking people simply throw up their hands and say, 'how could they do that?' Rosemary West's sexual abuse and murder of her daughter is undoubtedly one of the best examples.

Women, then, also figure prominently on the demand side of the equation of commercial sexual exploitation of children. There is more to the trade in child sex than a simple two-sided equation, however, for there is often a third party involved. Apart from the child who represents the supply and the client who provides the demand, there is a marketplace which is the domain of the procurer, recruiter, pimp, madam, friend or relative, these armies of intermediaries. Amongst these merchants of children's souls, there are many women.

Arranging the deal

In early 1996, Father Shay Cullen worked with a British television reporter to bring to European television audiences proof of the extent and nature of the formal child sex market in the Philippines. Armed with a hidden camera, Father Cullen posed as a potential client and arranged a meeting with the 'manager' of a bar in a seaside town that he knew to be a brothel where children could be bought. Unaware that she was being filmed, the woman explained to Cullen that he could take his pick of thirty or so girls kept in small cubicles upstairs , some as young as eight years old, for as little as US$3 (£2) a time. 'It's the cheapest fuck in the world,' she told him, oblivious to the fact that the children were paying with their dignity, their childhoods, their souls, maybe their lives.

The woman was an Australian, slim, attractive, in her late thirties or early forties who, in Cairns or Darwin or any other tropical Australian city, could have had a relaxed lifestyle running a beachside bar. It is impossible to understand why, instead, she would choose to make a living selling young children and live a life of criminality, corruption and deceit. In a voice devoid of any emotion, this woman explained to Shay Cullen how she was able to keep the bar going with the cooperation of the local police. The local chief of police, she said, owned a nearby mango farm. She regularly bought mangoes and used them for the fruit juices she sold in the bar. The police chief needed her custom, so he gave her his blessing. Thus, for the price of a few mangoes, she bought the cooperation she needed to be able to continue her filthy trade.

This Australian woman probably likes to see herself as an entrepreneur. She is a brothel madam, criminal and corrupt. She is one of a kind with the illiterate procurers who entice young children away from their villages with promises of work in the city or an education. These, too, are often women, traditionally 'aunties' who busy themselves with the affairs of the community and are trusted as members of the family even when they are not. All along the chains that shackle young girls and boys to a life in the commercial sex trade, there are women: mothers and older sisters and aunts and cousins who push the child to go out and earn a living for the sake of the family; recruiters and tricksters who take the girls away from homes which do not reject them but want to see them have a better life; brothel operators, madams who receive the girls and sell them to the highest bidder or, in time, whoever will take them.

And there are the men who bridge the gap between supply and demand: the pimps, procurers, kidnappers, thugs, club owners, street gang members, boyfriends, fathers and uncles.

Many of these merchants of death work alone or in small networks, although these can be highly structured and have outreach to other similar networks, often in other countries.

The Wood Commission in Australia in 1996 heard evidence of an Australian paedophile ring which operated in New South Wales in the 1970s and 1980s, and which was centred around Tony Bevan, a former Lord Mayor of Wollongong.[29] The network, which recruited boys in the King's Cross area of Sydney, involved several 'prominent people' including former politicians and people in local government. Boys were trafficked interstate, following 'orders' for them received by telex. Payments arriving by mail were known in the ring as 'royal mail'.

At the centre of the business, Bevan and a group of paedophile friends would meet at a nightclub called Costellos. Upstairs there were cubicles where the men could have sex with young boys, some as young as ten or 11. Most of the boys were runaways, homeless children picked up from the streets or parks around Sydney. They were handed around the men and sexually abused. Several of them, now grown men, gave evidence to the Wood Commission, telling of how they were often drugged and raped. They were also incited to bring new boys to the club. Although some of the boys eventually readjusted to normal lives, some had committed suicide and others had gone on to commit serious crimes. Among these were the three Murphy brothers who gained notoriety in Australia for raping and killing a nurse, Anita Colby.

Bevan kept detailed records, among them taped phone calls identifying 15 known Australian paedophiles and the numbers of corrupt officials in the Philippines. From these the Commission was able to learn how the New

South Wales ring supplied Australian and Filipino boys to other clients at home and overseas. As a former Lord Mayor, Bevan had high-placed friends and seemed untouchable. Corrupt members of the New South Wales police would alert Costellos nightclub when a raid was likely, and the boys would be hidden.

Despite enquiries and allegations over more than ten years about his exploitation, procurement, prostituting and trafficking of young children, Tony Bevan died in 1991 without ever being brought to justice.

The Tony Bevans of this world and their intimate little clubs which reach out to other like-minded people, and the 'hands-off' sham adoption and marriage agencies hiding behind respectable high street shopfronts, are the 'cottage industries' of commercial sexual exploitation of children. They are more organised than individual pimps and procurers and are helped and protected by well-placed contacts amongst the police, local authorities, and customs services. They are small fry, though, compared to the large criminal organisations which seem increasingly to be moving in on this lucrative trade in young flesh, veritable mafias of criminals whose business is diverse and for whom the trade in children's bodies may be only part of a portfolio of criminal activities. These international criminal organisations run parallel to and are set up along the same lines and routes as the trade in drugs, stolen cars and arms. They benefit from the fact that laws against commercial sexual exploitation of children have not yet caught up with those against other forms of trafficking. 'The risks for a trafficker to sell children or women for sexual purposes', according to Anita Gradin, European Commissioner, 'are lower than for smuggling drugs ... The sale and trafficking of children and women is [nevertheless] linked to other criminal activities. These include bribery and abduction, false identification and documentation, false marriages and adoptions, illegal immigration, violence and bonded labour. Linked to this are other severe problems, such as drugs, extortion and even homicide.'[30] These organised international criminal gangs are the most frightening adversaries of all, beyond the experience of the child rights agencies who have hitherto done most of the investigative work in the field of commercial sexual exploitation of children. They operate on a global scale, moving children from country to country to fulfil shifting demand, and their business is a multi-billion-dollar industry.

An October 1995 report commissioned by UNICEF [31] details some of the organised trafficking centred on Thailand:

> Thailand is a key transit point for illegal immigrants and migrant women and girls from Burma, Laos and China to third countries like Malaysia, Singapore, Japan or the United States, according to reports by Chiang Rai province police investigators ... Many, especially Chinese women and girls, are sent on to enter the flesh trade in Singapore and Malaysia. Many others are sent to Australia, New Zealand, Japan,

Taiwan, Germany and other European countries, the US and anywhere else where there is a demand for women and girls in the sex industry. The traffickers are not just confined to Thai, Burmese and Chinese gangsters. There are also many foreign criminals involved in the international trade in women and girls.

Other routes in Asia along which exploited children are trafficked include: Burma, Laos, Cambodia and Vietnam to Thailand; southern China to Thailand via Burma; internally within Thailand (rural to urban). Then, from Thailand many of these children will join Thai children and be moved on to China, Malaysia and Singapore. Children from Thailand and the Philippines are trafficked to Australia, New Zealand, Taiwan, Japan, Hong Kong, Sabah, Malaysia. Taiwanese children end up in Japan. Nepalese and Bangladeshi girls are sold to the brothels of India and Pakistan, and some are moved on, with Indian children, to the Middle East. Children from the South East Asian region also end up in Europe.[32]

Other trafficking routes operate from Latin America to Europe and the Middle East, from West Africa to the Middle East and Europe, and there are established routes in the Arab regional market and within Europe.[33]

Most of the trafficking in Europe in the late nineties originates in the eastern states, and is generally towards the west. Girls from Russia, the Ukraine and White Russia are transported in significant numbers to Poland, Hungary and the Baltic States, and many are them moved on to Western European capitals, joined by girls from bordering countries. Girls from Romania have been found in Italy, Cyprus and Turkey.

For these trafficking operations to work effectively and safely, there has to be corruption among the agencies whose professions and industries officially operate these international routes: airline companies, travel agencies, customs and immigration services, cargo handlers, border guards, police and law enforcement agencies. On 18 and 19 February 1991, the Crime Suppression Division of the Thai police arrested 15 employees of Thai Airways International (THAI) and charged them with falsifying documents and procuring women and girls for prostitution overseas. The workers used their status as THAI employees to obtain visas from foreign embassies, ostensibly for their 'wives and daughters'. They had allegedly substituted photographs of the trafficked women and girls into the passports of their own female family members, so that the young women could travel to Japan, where they would be prostituted. THAI was quick to point out that the alleged offenders were 'junior clerks' and that no higher authority had sanctioned their deception.

There are also, of course, the truck and bus drivers who transport shipments of young girls across land borders, and the hotel owners, receptionists, managers and other service providers who, in exchange for money, turn a blind eye to girls being moved into their premises for short stays. 'The truth is that sexual exploitation of children is a crime led by depraved and irresponsible sexual behaviour ... compounded by those entrepreneurs – individuals or members of national, transnational or international criminal networks – who have made a business out of it.'[34]

Alerting the many right-thinking people who are also part of the networks through which children are trafficked is one way to begin to stop the global trade in children. The story is told of Ameena, who would have been the victim of a child trafficker if not for the brave actions of one woman. Ameena boarded an Air India flight for Saudi Arabia in October 1991. The 11-year-old was accompanied by a 60-year-old Arab named Yahya As-Sagih. It was not a pleasant flight and a female cabin attendant of the Air India crew noticed that Ameena seemed to be distressed. She asked her in her own language what was wrong. Ameena, in tears, explained that she had been sold to the man she was travelling with and was being taken to Saudi Arabia against her will. Still speaking in a language the Arab could not understand, the attendant explained what had happened to other passengers on the flight and asked them to sign a petition calling for Ameena to be helped. She then alerted ground staff in New Delhi and, when the plane landed, As-Sagih was taken into custody. He had paid £150 for Ameena, the fourth young girl he had married in six months. Because he had a legal marriage licence, he was released. Ameena was returned to her family, who said they could not afford to keep her and so would sell her again. We do not know what eventually became of Ameena, but many young Indian girls do end up in Saudi Arabia, where they are sold again into the sex trade or as domestic servants. There are large markets in Bombay, Hyderabad and elsewhere in India where Arab customers can buy child brides whose virginity they value. With modern surgical techniques, however, hymens can be reconstructed and small containers of blood inserted into a young girl's vagina so that she can be sold as a virgin long after she has been deflowered. Potentially several times.

Playing a part

The actions of individuals, though, can clearly interrupt the flow of children being trafficked into slavery of one form or another. The actions of individual national organisations, professions or workplaces can also disrupt the lucrative trade. Steve Best, Chief Investigation Officer of the New Zealand Customs Service, is well aware of the potential of national customs officers to become active players in the campaign to end commercial sexual exploitation of children.[35] Best set up the Child Pornography Project within the New Zealand customs service as part of that country's national plan of action for children. The project aims not only to work against child pornography but to work with police, international counterparts and other players to coordinate action against those who exploit children for sex. In the course of screening international mail, New Zealand Customs intercepted five black and white photographs of naked Asian boys in pornographic poses. An accompanying letter postmarked Sydney, Australia, led the officers to believe that the person to whom the photos were addressed had done business with the sender before and that the sender was supplying such materials to customers in other countries. In other words, they had stumbled upon an international pornography distributor.

The Customs officers alerted New Zealand police, obtained a search warrant and, with the police, confronted the customer at home. He admitted that he had requested the photos, that he knew the boys depicted were under-age, and said he wanted the photos only for personal gratification. He pleaded guilty to a charge of importing prohibited goods, but asked for leniency on the grounds that the pornography was intended 'to keep children safe from me'. The judge was not convinced: he convicted and fined him.

During the search of the customer's home, moreover, police had found evidence that he was a regular companion to intellectually disabled children. They found a letter from a charitable organisation working with such children thanking him for volunteering to take the children on outings. The organisation had no idea of his paedophilia but was speedily alerted to it.

And there was more. Copies of the letter and photographs were passed to the Australian Customs Service. With New South Wales state police officers, Australian customs officers began investigating the Sydney-based supplier of the pornographic materials. He had used a false name in his dealings with the New Zealand customer but, following police stake-out of his post office box, he was identified. It transpired that he was already under surveillance by New South Wales police but lack of evidence meant they had not been able to secure a search warrant. Now, armed with the letter and photographs from New Zealand, they were able to obtain a warrant and search his premises. They found the nerve-centre of a major child porn production and distribution business. Police seized more than 7000 negatives and a list of more than 80 clients in Australia and overseas. Customs services in all the countries to which he had been sending orders for these clients were notified. Five black and white photographs – and the vigilance of the New Zealand Customs Service – were the key to a number of international paedophile rings exploiting children through pornography.

As globalisation becomes the buzz-word of the end of the twentieth century, the infrastructure, both human and capital, involved in the commercial sexual exploitation of children is growing at a phenomenal rate. In his opening statement to the Stockholm Congress in August 1996, Ron O'Grady warned:

> One of the most significant features of the twenty-first century will certainly be a massive move towards globalisation. The signs are everywhere evident: the

commercial world speaks with enthusiasm of world trade and an open market. The tourism industry is predicting a dramatic increase in the number of people travelling to all parts of the planet. Above all, the explosion in the communications industry and the emerging impact of the Internet and satellite transmission has begun to challenge us in a new way with both the advantages and the dangers of a world without borders. A united world is a very utopian proposition and it is one of many attractive aspects to globalisation. It is an inspiring vision to speak of a new unity among humankind in the twenty-first century with its hope for a better world of peace and justice. But nothing is simple and there is a down-side to globalisation. It is one of the negative consequences of developing globalism which has brought us together in this Congress: children have become casualties on the march to a global society.[36]

If the criminals who sexually exploit children grow big-time and establish international networks to conduct their business, then the child rights organisations will have to do the same. Although at times the size and scope of the problem of children being sold and bought for sex seems daunting, there is little doubt that the actions being taken against this criminal trade can match up. In recent years, campaigns, specific actions, legal amendments, law enforcement moves, public information pressure, lobbying and physical interventions have grown in size and frequency. What is needed now is a bringing-together of these disjointed, disparate efforts into global action against the commercial sexual exploitation of children. The first steps have already been taken.

5 Is anybody out there doing anything? What can be done to fight it

In August 1996, government representatives from 122 countries, 105 delegates from United Nations and other intergovernmental agencies, 471 representatives from non-governmental organisations, 47 youth delegates and organisers, and 538 members of the world's media came together in Stockholm, Sweden, to give the clearest sign yet that the people who sexually exploit children have a battle on their hands.

The first World Congress against Commercial Sexual Exploitation of Children was a unique meeting from day one. First of all, it was not a normal United Nations/government conference, at which other players had to be content to observe. The Stockholm Congress was co-sponsored by the Swedish Government, UNICEF, the ECPAT campaign and the NGO Group for the Convention on the Rights of the Child. Government, UN and NGO players therefore came to the forum as equal partners – an important innovation, reflecting the fact that the commercial sexual exploitation of children has to be fought on a number of different fronts simultaneously and in different ways depending on the special skills of the individuals and organisations involved. Xavier Emmanuelli, then French Secretary of State for Humanitarian Relief, was to highlight this after the Congress when he addressed key players in France's contribution to the fight, '[there is] one strategy,' he said. 'Against the networks of exploiters, we must put up networks of all those who are able to act.'

Governments and the law

Principal players among those who can make a difference are governments. In their hands lies the ability to review laws covering not only protection of children against commercial sexual exploitation, but also criminalisation of pornography and punishment of exploiters – both the intermediaries and those who buy children for sex. They are also necessarily responsible for national and ultimately international action to seek out the perpetrators of child sex and bring them to justice.

Most countries do have laws making sexual abuse of children, kidnapping, enslavement, and the sale and trafficking of children a crime. Additionally, 191 countries (at 30 June 1997) have signed and ratified the United Nations *Convention on the Rights of the Child*, Article 34 of which commits governments to work against commercial sexual exploitation of children. Indeed, there is a whole host of international treaties and support mechanisms to them that could be applied in the fight to prevent children from being bought and sold for sex but, as Thomas Hammarberg, former member of the United Nations Committee for the Rights of the Child, has written, 'The machineries which have been established, including the UN Committee on the Rights of the Child and the UN Special Rapporteur, still have to prove that they can contribute to decisive action against sexual exploitation of children.'[1] The treaties date from as early as 1904, when governments agreed to the *International Agreement for the Suppression of White Slave Traffic* – which would include, for example, children being trafficked across borders into brothels or paedophile rings. They include treaties covering slavery, trafficking, pornography, prostitution, forced labour, a minimum age for economic activity, refugee protection, sexual crimes in warfare, discrimination against women and, in 1989, the *Convention on the Rights of the Child* itself.[2] Although these are commonly seen as 'soft law' because they do not exist, as such, on the legal statute books of countries, they nevertheless are binding and can be used as the foundation for action. The *Convention on the Rights of the Child* also has a monitoring mechanism written into it – the Committee on the Rights of the Child – to which States Parties are supposed to report regularly on the progress they have made towards implementing the Convention. Few countries have so far reported.

Even 'hard laws' which have been put in place, however, are not standard across the board and, in particular, the age of the young people targeted by them differs from country to country. Laws against child pornography are a good example: while production and distribution of pornography involving children is an offence in most countries, possession is not always an offence and, in countries where it is not illegal, it is consequently impossible to arrest the person in possession, impound the materials and investigate with a view to weeding out the producers and hence identifying the exploiters. Differences among national laws within a region mean that exploiters can move children or operations across borders and often escape arrest.

In the wake of the Stockholm Congress, though, governments began co-operating more urgently to move towards standardisation of national legislation governing commercial sexual exploitation of children. European justice ministers, for example, met in Dublin, Ireland, in September 1996 and began a review of European laws, announcing, in late November, that they were finalising handing over to Europol, the European grouping of law enforcement agencies whose mandate already covered drug trafficking and money laundering, the responsibility to track movement in children for sexual purposes. This European Union counterpart of the international police organisation Interpol will work in cooperation with is global partner to 'increase effectiveness in tackling crime against minors and [lead to] the more efficient use of resources within both organisations', according to Interpol head Raymond Kendall.[3] Interpol has already stepped up its fight against the sexual exploitation of children, developing computer databases recording details of sex offenders and missing children. In late 1996 a project was initiated on paedophile networks and international sales of child pornography.

In February 1997, the Council of the European Union adopted a 'joint action'[4] requiring member states of the Union to review 'existing laws and practice' with a view to combating sexual exploitation of children. In mid-1997, the European Commission launched its DAPHNE Initiative, a funding mechanism to encourage European NGOs to work together to fight sexual violence against children.

Making the law work

Beyond legislation, the enforcement of laws – both existing and newly created – is also coming under review. Interpol has a Standing Working Party on Offences against Minors, which includes representatives not only of national law enforcement agencies but also non-governmental organisations and UNICEF. Interpol has been active in promoting extraterritorial legislation and in helping its members to cooperate to make sure that it functions effectively. Members of the British police force, for example, have trained Philippines police in identifying sex exploiters and collecting evidence which will stand up in court either in the Philippines or overseas, and Australian and Swedish police have both worked closely with law enforcement bodies in Thailand, to investigate nationals of their countries reported to be operating in Thai jurisdiction.

More and more countries are looking at the introduction and enforcement of extraterritoriality laws. By mid-1997, 12 countries – Sweden, Norway, Denmark, Finland, Iceland, France, Belgium, Germany, Australia, New Zealand, Canada and the United States – had already enacted laws which allow them to pursue their citizens (and sometimes non-citizen residents of their country) for sex exploitation crimes committed in other countries, and several more were in the process of passing such legislation or amending Penal Codes to allow extraterritoriality.

Among the extraterritoriality laws which exist at the moment, however, there are some inconsistencies. It has proven very difficult to get judges to understand how hard it is for a young child who has been exploited to stand up and talk about it in a foreign court. Not only are there problems of language and unfamiliarity with the surroundings; the victims of sexual exploitation have suffered severe trauma and are often torn between exploiter and family offering them incentives to tell one story and child rights organisations encouraging them to speak out. They may have formed an attachment to the person who has been exploiting them, confused by gifts they were given and promises still outstanding, and may not know what awaits them if the person is sent to jail.

This was a problem under French extraterritoriality law.[5] Since 1 February 1994, French citizens who sexually exploit children overseas can be brought to justice in France. After the Stockholm Congress, however, in November 1996, French extraterritoriality law was strengthened to take into account not just acts involving children overseas engaged in prostitution but all sexual offences against minors, with or without remuneration. It was also expanded to outlaw businesses promoting sex tourism – an important step to cut off facilities for sex tourists at home – and to include offences committed by foreigners resident on French soil.

Australian extraterritoriality laws have avoided some of the pitfalls. They both recognise the reality and the special needs of children who have been exploited, and allow for the child's testimony to be given via video linking, so that the child can give evidence without travelling to a foreign and strange environment. This is now being considered in a number of other countries. Australian laws also accept alternative methods of determining the age of the child where there is doubt. The same laws contain a forfeiture provision which allows for confiscation of property used in the committing of a crime, and this can be a strong deterrent to tour operators and allied businesses involved in facilitating child sex tourism.[6] Indeed, extraterritoriality law in general has been shown to be a strong deterrent against indiscriminate, as opposed to highly organised, child sex tourism. If a group of young Australian men on holiday in Asia think it might be 'fun' to pick up under-age girls for sex, they now know that the law can follow them home and they could find themselves in prison in Australia and hounded by the Australian media. Publicity of arrests and convictions under extraterritoriality law and, indeed, under national laws in the country where the crime has been committed, is also a strong deterrent.

Another initiative which helps the enforcement of extraterritoriality laws is the establishment of bilateral treaties between nations, accompanied by the setting up of mechanisms such as liaison officer posts in the countries which receive child sex tourists. Sweden, Norway, Denmark and Finland have created a Nordic countries' liaison officer in South East Asia. Where such an initiative has not been possible because of financial constraints, then training of diplomatic and embassy personnel stationed overseas is a realistic alternative. In fact, awareness-raising among diplomatic staff is an important element in preventative and punitive action, given the disturbing fact that more and more diplomats are being identified as exploiters and brought to justice. Importantly, embassy staff need to be supported when they do have evidence of exploiters in their midst, and not hamstrung by fears that such knowledge will bring the embassy or the country of origin into disrepute.

There is also much awareness-raising to do amongst those whose job it is to enforce the law: the police and local authorities. From England, where Crime Squad officers mocked the bruises on the young Dawn Shields's battered face, to the Philippines where a local police chief took blood money for mangoes, the police have to learn what the commercial sexual exploitation of children means – not only to the children, but to society as a whole and to our future. As Javier Perez de Cuellar, former United Nations Secretary-General, said, 'The way a society treats children reflects not only its qualities of compassion and protective caring but also its sense of justice, its commitment to the future and its urge to enhance the human condition for coming generations.'

The people who are responsible for law enforcement officers also have to start making them accountable for the children on their beats. Police officers and other law enforcement personnel are exploited children's first line of defence. Children must be able to turn to them for help, not see them as partners of the very people who are exploiting them.

And this is not just a so-called Third World problem. Although it is undoubtedly true that police in Asia, South America and Africa have among them corrupt officers who cooperate with exploiters for their own financial gain, police in the industrialised world whose inflexibility and often sheer thoughtlessness keep young children in servitude also have a lot to learn. Law enforcement officers who disregard obvious signs of abuse, react to a plea for help by simply taking a statement and then returning the child to the people who are exploiting her, or carelessly let exploiters know that a child has spoken out against them without acting to protect the child at the same time, are increasing the likelihood that the child will be moved on, beaten into submission or even killed.

'Even though it is not possible to make a racehorse out of a pig,' Interpol's Ann Kristin-Olsen told delegates at a law enforcement meeting in Bangkok,[7] 'it is possible to make a faster pig. Law enforcement can change.' And there are signs that this is happening. Several police forces have now set up special child protection units who not only have a specific mandate to oversee action related to children, but also raise awareness and skills within the ranks of their own forces.

Victimising the victims

One area where this is particularly important is in the attitude police have to the children who are exploited. Between 1989 and 1993 in England and Wales, for example, 1500 convictions were secured against children for offences relating to prostitution. The children were labelled as 'criminals'. What about the men who were buying sex from them? Or the pimps who were keeping them as virtual slaves? Or the families who may have turned them out on to the streets in the first place? Law enforcers need to be helped and encouraged to see beyond the letter of the law to the spirit of the laws against under-age sex, to realise who the real criminals are.

In other parts of the world, children found in brothels, massage parlours or on the streets are regularly rounded up and deported, finding themselves back in the place from which they were sold or with nowhere to go at all. Many of these children, too, are locked in holding cells with adult prisoners, who may abuse them sexually.[8] It is little wonder that many of these children, when they are free, simply return to the brothels or clubs they were freed from, where at least they may know other children and have a roof over their heads.

But is it fair to expect the average police officer to be aware of all these issues? Child rights workers think it is fair, but that they need help and support. With this in mind, the United States Department of Justice compiled for its law enforcement officers a 'blueprint for action' designed to help them understand the myriad issues involved when a young child is found in prostitution. The blueprint gives the example of a young girl arrested during a routine sweep for prostitution, whose identification papers seemed to have been altered:

> Upon questioning, the girl admitted that she was 15 years of age and had been given a forged driver's license by her boyfriend. The boyfriend, who was 32 years of age, was arrested when he came to the precinct house to post bail for the girl. A check of his arrest record revealed that he had a criminal record for minor drug charges and breaking-and-entering in a neighbouring state. Additional questioning of the girl revealed that she had met the man ... after she ran away from home. He had convinced her that easy money could be made through prostitution and had paid for her bus ticket to the city in which the arrest was made. Because state lines had been crossed, the US Attorney's Office and the FBI were notified. Given the girl's age and history, a decision was made (and approved by the local prosecutor) not to prosecute her on the prostitution charge if she would testify against her pimp on the federal charges. However, a records check revealed that the girl was a ward of the court in her city of origin, and had a history of running away from home, public drunkenness and minor drug offences ... the girl was placed in secure detention until arrangements could be made to return her to the Division of Youth Services in her home state. Upon hearing [this] the girl alleged that she had

run away from home because of sexual abuse by her stepfather. A report of these allegations was forwarded to both the Division of Youth Services and the Police Department in her city of origin. There, the police filed a report with the child protection agency which convened a multidisciplinary child abuse team to investigate the charges. The child protection agency arranged to place the girl in foster care upon her return to her city of origin. Meanwhile, the US Attorney's Office was preparing its case against the boyfriend. The Victim/Witness Coordinator in the US Attorney's Office worked closely with the Victim Assistance Unit of the local prosecutor's office to arrange support services for the girl when she returned to testify against her pimp. The Victim Assistance Officer in her city of origin, which has a representative on the multidisciplinary child abuse team, provided similar services during all proceedings involving the stepfather. The juvenile court in that city deferred action on the charges involving theft of the car until the child abuse charges were resolved.[9]

What this example clearly shows is how complex a 'simple' case of child sexual exploitation can be. In this one investigation, several different issues came into play: forged documents, a runaway ward of court, car theft, potential sexual abuse in the home, prostitution of a minor, pimping. And several different agencies worked together both to see that justice was done and also to protect the young girl involved: the original police investigators, the US Attorney's Office, the FBI, the Division of Youth Services, the Victim/Witness Coordinator and two separate Victim Assistance Units. What the US Department of Justice chose to draw out for the advice of its law enforcement officers were the fact that the young girl had potentially been abused at home, her criminal record which might be used by defence counsel to undermine any evidence she would eventually give, the girl's attachment to her 'boyfriend' and the conflict this would cause her in giving evidence, her long-term needs as a runaway and the need to give her protection and provide secure long-term accommodation for her. This 'best interests of the child' approach may be time-consuming and complex, but it ultimately ensures that criminals, not their child victims, are targeted, and that is surely what laws are for and what law enforcement officers strive to achieve.

On 19 March 1996, the Royal Thai Government informed the world's press that its Cabinet had approved 'specific legislation against the prostitution of minors', in the form of a new Prevention and Suppression of Prostitution Act. Under this, no penalties would be stipulated for children found working in prostitution, since they are considered 'victims of the illegal sex trade'. Instead, the press release states, 'customers and procurers, not the victims, should face punishment'.[10]

Avoiding re-victimising the victim is an important step forward in the battle against commercial sexual exploitation of children, because it puts the best interests of the child at the centre of action being taken, and signals at last that the emphasis of blame is shifting away from the children to the criminals who exploit them. Some members of the media have still to catch up with this shift.

What the papers say

How many times have you picked up a news magazine carrying an article about children being sold for sex, or about sex tourists exploiting children in some Asian country, and seen a gruesome picture of a grown man man-handling a frail girl-child? And how many times has the man's face been masked, shaded or otherwise disguised to protect his identity? Now how many times has the child's face been covered to protect her identity? Time and time again, newspaper editors, television producers and photo editors on glossy magazines have been careful to protect the identity of the exploiter – sometimes for legal reasons but often also from a knee-jerk 'protection' instinct – and reveal the face of the exploited. The argument for this is invariably the same: 'We need to show the child's eyes so that people can sympathise with her. You want people to sympathise, don't you?' Of course we do. But not at the sake of her dignity.

Sometimes the argument has been contradictory: 'We didn't hide the child's eyes because it makes her look like a criminal.' Although in recent times a number of major news outlets have considered this problem in-house and issued loose guidelines on child protection, the debate continues. It will do so as long as so-called 'scandal sheets' or even photo editors who simply don't see a 13-year-old 'go-go' dancer in a bar as a child needing protection, victimise the victim in the pages of their papers. Perhaps the only solution is to encourage photographers to take photographs in the first instance which show the exploiter full face but picture the child in such a way that her dignity remains intact: perhaps with her back to the camera, with her face in shadows, or from a high enough angle that her face cannot be seen. A little imagination and a much greater understanding of the issues involved – the child's dignity and the exploiter's criminality – would surely lead to usable pictures.

The visual media have been criticised, too, for insensitivity in selecting photographs they use to illustrate stories about children caught in prostitution. Photographs of children who are working on the streets, for example, include children who are not necessarily selling sex. Yet often the caption that accompanies the photo labels the street children in the shot as 'child prostitutes'. Conversely, there was controversy in mid-1996 when a German television station showed images of a German man with two Asian children on a beach and suggested in the commentary that this was a child sex tourist with his prey; it turned out that the man was a father spending a day at the beach with his two children. He sued.

Criticism of media coverage of the issue of commercial sexual exploitation of children, though, has to be considered alongside the fact that the media are major players in the fight to end the selling of children for sex. Investigative reporters have shown great determination and skill in undercover investigations, often in collaboration with non-governmental organisations, and have helped in the conviction of exploiters. At the same time, there have been cases where reports have been put to air while an investigation was under way, alerting the exploiters to the fact that they were being observed and compromising evidence in the process. In short, just as law enforcement and diplomatic staff can benefit from awareness-raising and training, so too could media professionals: reporters, editors, photo editors and those who commission stories.

The Stockholm Congress was strongly in favour of self-regulation for media workers, rather than rules and regulations imposed from outside the profession. Aidan White, Secretary-General of the International Federation of Journalists, led the discussion of how journalists' codes of ethics and training could be reviewed to help them understand more fully the importance of child rights and the issues involved in reporting commercial sexual exploitation of children. At the same time, workers in child rights have a lot to learn about the media. Expectations of the press by many agencies are unrealistic, the Congress heard, with non-governmental organisations sometimes believing that the press are propaganda machines which can be manipulated in the interests of a 'good cause'. Perhaps the most promising sign that came out of the Stockholm Congress was the overwhelming interest of the world's press to come to grips with the issue of commercial sexual exploitation of children, to understand it in all its depth and complexity and to report its horrors to the public in the best way they can. There is no doubt, in fact, that the work being done in the press rooms at the Stockholm Congress, which resulted in daily coverage of the issue of commercial sexual exploitation of children and was invaluable in raising public awareness of the topic, was itself a major contribution to the campaign to stop children being exploited for sex. There is also no doubt that mistakes will continue to be made. Some journalists will still publish the addresses of brothels selling under-age children. Some photo editors will still choose pictures of beaches where sex tourism is flourishing – and name the beach so that prospective exploiters know exactly where to go. Many reports will still compromise the dignity of the child and leave the exploiter untouched. But the tide has turned in media reporting of commercial sexual exploitation of children, and governments, law enforcement agencies, UN agencies and exploiters themselves can now be sure that the eyes of the world's press, along with the NGOs – those 'policemen of the humanitarian world' – are also firmly fixed on what they are doing, and that they will be called to account for their actions on the front pages of newspapers, and in the headlines of radio and television news reports.

Beyond the reporting of sexual exploitation of children, however, the media have a much more complex and controversial role to play. In today's world, television, radio, advertising, computer information vehicles, newspapers and other mass media are instrumental in forming not only children's views of sex and childhood, not only adult views of sex and children, but everyone's views of society, morality, good and evil. 'Comic books, music television and the Internet are the newspapers of the new generation,' an MTV journalist told the Stockholm Congress.[11] The Lolita and Beavis and Butthead syndromes, which deal directly with the image of the child and which many people believe may warp that image and send out confusing messages to children and the adults seeking justification for exploiting them, are just the tip of the iceberg.

Today's media leave no stones unturned in their treatment of all the issues that coalesce to mould the fantasies and realities of modern society: family, education, war and conflict, the arts, science, nature, sex, money, relationships – to complete the list would be to describe life itself. While the media often claim to be a simple mirror of society, they have the technical and artistic means to be at the leading edge of that society and to nudge it along the path. The media help to make us what we are and contribute both to forming and consolidating the values and attitudes we live by. So how can they help us to value and protect our children better? How can they help children to see that their bodies are priceless and that abuse of them by anyone, even someone who promises them great gifts in return, is wrong?

There is no simple answer to this question. Certainly the media can involve young people in the making and presenting of programmes, so that their voice is heard and their value to society is shown. 'The choice – and voice – of the child are the key to not only knowing how to talk to children but also to learning how to talk about children,' the Stockholm Congress heard.[12] Equally importantly, those who create images and the contexts – both verbal and visual – in which these images are interpreted, can include children in their reaction tests of the messages they are sending out. What will a 13-year-old think when she sees a billboard showing a child-like model draped naked across a couch with an adult man bending over her? She may just think this is a strange way to advertise lipstick. She may think that what her abusive uncle told her last night about grown men having sex with young girls being 'normal' is true, after all. And what about the paedophile who drives past in his car? What are we saying to him?

This is just one example, and the whole debate about what is right and wrong, suitable and unsuitable, clever and dangerous, risky and harmless, will rage on. The media will – and do – argue that they are not ultimately responsible for protecting children, that this is the job of parents, schoolteachers, priests. But such arguments must be taken in the context of a wider society which has to a large extent cast aside its responsibility for children.

Schools claim that parents are responsible; parents say that schools could do more; both of these blame the church for not giving enough moral guidance; everyone blames the media. The truth is that these collective groupings comprise many millions of individual people. If each parent, each school-teacher, each priest and each individual journalist or media worker stopped to think about the way their actions impact upon children, individually and collectively, and took responsibility for their own actions, then children would begin to receive the protection they need to keep them from falling into the trap of under-age sex, and the ultimate trap of being forced to sell it by someone else. 'If we want to end the sexual exploitation of children,' UNICEF Executive Director Carol Bellamy told the Stockholm Congress, 'we must combat it in private as well as in the public sphere.'[13]

In this regard, many journalists have pointed out that, while they are part of 'the media', they are also human beings with individual responsibilities which, as much as any other member of society, they take seriously. They are also often parents, with children of their own, and are not, as some critics of the press sometimes seem to think, totally divorced from the realities of children and life in general.

The media – all forms of media, from television reporters to advertising creative staff to Internet web page producers – are set to continue to make their unique and important contribution both to the fight against commercial sexual exploitation of children and to the debate on values which lies at the heart of how we view the child. This needs to be done in conjunction with debate on the ethics codes and commercial pressures which govern the media's work. As the Stockholm Congress panel debate on the role of the media concluded, 'Ultimately, the media's responsibility is to steer a course which allows them to provide reliable, ethical, accurate reports without being at the bidding of any interest group – this independence is funda-mental to free, democratic media and consequently therefore to protecting the rights of children.'[14] The answer does not lie in regulation of the media, but in 'self-regulation, increased professionalism, greater awareness and formal and informal monitoring mechanisms' as well as realistic cooperation between the media and those who can help them understand the issues surrounding the rights of the child and specific infringements of them, such as commercial sexual exploitation. The Congress discussion on the role the media can play in the fight against child sex resulted in a number of recom-mendations:

1. The 'best interests of the child' as embodied in the Convention on the Rights of the Child are the ultimate test of appropriateness in the work of both the media and information professionals in agencies concerned with child rights. If this is internalised, then many of the problems will be solved. UNICEF and non-govern-mental organisations have a responsibility to promote understanding of the Convention by media professionals and to help them to integrate it into their work

and into the ethical conducts they apply to their professional activity. News media organisations should consider appointing specialist correspondents with a specific responsibility for children's issues.

2.   Codes of Ethics, rather than imposed regulation, are the key to improving the output of the media in reporting and presenting issues concerning and of concern to children. UNICEF and NGOs can work with media professionals to ensure that children's issues are integrated into the personal and professional ethics of those in the media professions. Such cooperation can take the form of collaborative training courses, training materials, workshops, meetings and ongoing discussion. Children themselves should be included in such cooperative work.

3.   Access of children to the media is also vital. Not only must their voice be heard, they must also be helped to become critical audiences of the various media. It is the responsibility of adults both to facilitate access of children to the media and to help children to interpret the messages of the media.

4.   Media professionals and the associations which represent them must focus on the need for ethical conduct. This is best done by self-regulation and the flexibility which allows each individual case to be the basis for ethical decision-making. Mechanisms such as Codes of Ethics, professional associations, press councils and children's ombudsmen should be promoted in order to underpin self-regulation and monitor its effectiveness.

5.   Those who work in the arena of child rights must learn how the media work in order to understand the constraints media face and ensure that these do not stand in the way of appropriate reporting and image-building. This is the responsibility of UNICEF and NGOs who wish to tap the potential of the media. Increased professionalism can be encouraged by such projects as ongoing training of information and press staff, guidelines for dealing with the media, identification and training of spokespersons who face the press, careful formulation and monitoring of the messages and improved collection of reliable data being given to the press.

6.   NGOs and UN agencies must provide accurate, verifiable information and not distort in order to sell a story to the press. By proving themselves to be reliable sources of information with an agenda for truth rather than self-promotion, organisations can build solid working relationships with the media based on a shared concern for reporting the facts. It is time for UNICEF and NGOs to critically review the image they give of children to readers and viewers of diverse media. A well understood and circulated Code of Conduct for dealing with the press could be used for in-house training and policy guidance.

7.   Civil society must demand accuracy and ethical behaviour not only from the press but from children's organisations. The media, NGOs and UNICEF must be accountable for their work in informing about children's rights. In this respect, mechanisms such as encouraging appointment of a children's ombudsman could be explored.

8.   More serious research is needed to analyse how children are described in the media, what underlies such description and how it can be positively influenced in the interests of children. The issue of stereotyping of children in general and vulnerable children in particular should be further explored.

9.   The media can not only advocate on behalf of children but contribute to providing support services to help children help themselves. Services such as telephone help lines, educational programmes and awareness-raising campaigns are only possible with the support of other organisations, and consequently the media, UNICEF and NGOs must work together and identify or commit resources to providing these services.

10.   Parents must take responsibility for providing support to their children as consumers of the media. Parents can not only guide children as they develop as media consumers but provide additional context, explanation and diversity of sources of information to balance the impact of media and help the child to grow in understanding.

11.   The potential of all media – not just the news media – must not be forgotten. Books, films, comics, posters and other entertainment and performing arts can also be used in the promotion and reinforcement of child rights and children's issues. Organisations working for and with children should explore such avenues for promoting their message and as an outlet for children to make their voice heard.

12.   There must be internationally agreed standards of regulation governing the use and abuse of new communication technologies. These must cover the source, format, transmission and reception of information and must clearly define what is public and private space and provide nations with guidelines for the elimination of materials which are exploitative of children or likely to encourage such exploitation. Such an approach will require the establishment of a single international agency to coordinate activity in this field. The UN agencies, including UNICEF, must address the potential establishment of such an agency within the UN system as a matter of urgency.

These recommendations are worth repeating in detail because they illustrate so clearly how, even when the role of one sector of society is being discussed, the issue of children's rights, their exploitation, what underlies it and who can do something to help stop it, is complex and wide-ranging. Did you recognise yourself among the players listed as having a responsibility to do something? Think about it. Next time, for example, you see something in an advertisement, television programme or newspaper that you believe sends out a confusing message to children about their sexuality or their relationships with adults, do something about it. Write and complain. Take your concerns to a press council or advertising standards bureau. Most importantly, discuss it with your children, find out what they think, let them know your opinion, make them feel that they can discuss issues like this openly with you and support them as they form their opinions and their value-sets. Avoid, at all costs, giving way to the feeling that something you feel uncomfortable about is 'not really important' or that your children 'probably didn't notice it anyway'. A 1996 survey found that more than half of all primary school children in the United Kingdom have televisions in their bedrooms and 25 per cent have their own video recorders,[15] so it is more than likely that your children did notice. Take a few minutes to think about what your children see and hear in the media and share your thoughts with them. Listen to what they say, respect their opinions and clear the air so that both you and they know how you both feel about something potentially difficult and are satisfied – not necessarily in agreement – with each other's views. 'It is because we do not respect children in their individuality and fundamental human value that we still tend to minimise situations of sexual exploitation of children, including child pornography and prostitution.'[16]

Keeping tabs on tourism

There is another group of people who have a specific task in the fight against commercial sexual exploitation of children. This is the 'tourist industry', a diverse collection of individuals, small enterprises, big businesses, airlines, hotel chains and individual travellers who are their customers. Travel is an everyday part of life now. As Martin Staebler has pointed out, 'crossing a border has lost its magic for many people, thus making foreign and domestic travel in their minds more and more alike. However this does not change a basic reality, namely that travel to a foreign country is not a neutral action. International visitors should therefore enter a foreign country with sensitivity to cultural, ethnic, social, economic or religious differences between their country of origin and should respect the values that these differences entail in the host country. This is especially evident in sexual customs.'[17]

There are more specific ways and means, though, for the business side of the tourism and travel industries to enter the campaign against commercial sexual exploitation of children. The World Tourism Organisation (WTO), the Universal Federation of Travel Agents' Associations (UFTAA), the International Air Transport Association (IATA) and the International Union of Food, Agriculture, Hotel, Restaurant, Catering, Tobacco and Allied Workers Associations (IUF), among other groups, have all condemned the phenomenon of child sex tourism and for some time have been looking at ways to help stop it, including drafting charters which bind their members to work against child sex tourism. This is a pragmatic move as well as a moral one. Tourism is the life-blood of many people, top of the list in world exports and the leading tradable services sector, employing some 200 million people worldwide. The number of international tourist arrivals in 1995 was estimated at some 567 million; it is expected to increase to 967 million by the year 2010. Child sex tourism is damaging tourism's reputation.

As a result, several tourism organisations have formulated trade conventions which ensure that agencies which promote sex tours will lose their licence to trade as tour agents. Public pressure is important here, too. A Swiss journalist's exposé in 1992 of a sex tour he had taken after booking through a Swiss travel agent caused public uproar and led to the agency closing down.

It is not just a question of organising sex tours. Some agencies 'help' their customers by identifying places where they will be able to buy prostitutes – and often, therefore, exploited children – for sex. They negotiate deals with hotels to ensure that the client is not embarrassed when he tries to take someone back to his room for sex, and they provide local representatives who facilitate such behaviour.

Allied to this 'assisted sex tourism' are the guide books and travel publications that promote sex tourism explicitly or, quite often, inadvertently through careless writing or photo choice. The example is often quoted of the Lauda Air in-flight magazine which in 1992 carried a colourful feature article illustrated by a mock postcard from Asia. It showed a young Asian girl child, naked from the waist up, and the message 'Must go, the tarts in the Baby Club are waiting for me!' After complaints and a public row, the magazine was withdrawn. On the positive side, a number of major tour guide publishers have themselves entered the fight against commercial sexual exploitation of children. *Fodors,* one of the world's largest publishers of guide books, has a policy to avoid insensitive information that might aid exploiters, and *Lonely Planet*, the Australia-based company that specialises in upbeat guides for younger travellers, conducts awareness-raising exercises among its contributors so that they do not write materials that might facilitate the selling or buying of children for sex.

Many major airlines are also doing what they can to raise awareness about children being sold into sex to satisfy tourist demand and exploiters' greed, including showing short films on the subject in-flight, and distributing leaflets explaining the issues and, in countries where there are extraterritoriality laws, the possible consequences. Swedish Save the Children helped in the production of a clever card to be inserted by Swedish Travel Agency Association members into airline tickets to Asia. One side showed a glorious white beach – the 'bright side' of tourism; the other side was black, with an explanation of the 'dark side'. The French travel industry has also produced a leaflet, distributed through travel agencies or airlines and, in this way, many millions of people have become aware of child sex tourism. Australian Customs distributes a leaflet prepared by ECPAT Australia and New Zealand is planning to do the same. Garuda Indonesian airlines inserts a brochure into the seat pocket of its flights from Australia and America, containing a Code of Ethics for Travellers, and the Italian Federation of

Travel and Tourism is ready to do the same in conjunction with Alitalia airlines.

In March 1997 an international 'stop sex tourism' logo was launched to identify agencies and operators who declare themselves in the fight against sex tourism. That same month, a campaign was launched in Brazil called 'Beware, Brazil is watching you'. The theme of the campaign, which features a pair of alert, menacing eyes on promotional materials, was public protection of children from sex tourists. Campaign materials included information posters, advice on airline tickets and T-shirts with a telephone number to report potential incidents of exploitation.

While the organisations and companies involved in the tourist industry do seem to be making some headway in their contribution to attempts to end sexual exploitation of children, it should not be forgotten that many of the exploiters work on a much smaller scale, driving taxis, operating small brothels, offering children on street corners. Here again we are back at the level of individual values and individual action. What would you do if you saw a pimp obviously offering a 12-year-old child to a foreign tourist? Would you confront them? Report them? Photograph them? Follow them and try and stop them? What if someone you know has exploited a child?

A French tour group arrived in Pattaya, Thailand, in 1992. Among them were two young male friends sharing a room. One of them bought a young boy for sex. His friend reported him to the local police and the exploiter was deported.[18] It was the end of a friendship but one less case of sexual exploitation of a child. One drop in an ocean, but then an ocean is in any case just a very large collection of drops.

Taking such action may carry risks with it and, if you do feel strongly enough to intervene, then you should certainly think through these risks and reduce them as far as possible – for example by asking help from other outraged travellers, the police or official representatives. It is a good thing, though, to be aware of what is happening around you and to open your eyes to instances where children are being exploited. Many people would be outraged, for example, to know that some of the men who travel on sex tours do so at the expense of their companies as a 'thank you' for a job well done. If you found out that this was happening in your company, you would be fully justified in gathering support around you and complaining to management. Remember, also, if management is uncooperative, that the media are extremely interested in the issue of sex tourism . . .

Values and attitudes

Ron O'Grady has written, 'change will only occur when there is a strong sense of moral outrage in the community at the sexual abuse of children and when the community as a whole embraces common transcendent values and goals which can be described as "spiritual". These include the sacredness of the life of the young child and respect by adults for the rights of the child.'[19] While O'Grady sees this as a challenge to the leaders of religious communities, it is surely also a challenge to everyone in civil society, religious beliefs or not. In fact, as O'Grady also points out, religions have a poor track record in dealing with human sexuality and sexual attitudes towards children. 'The evidence for this', he writes, 'is partly seen in the number of apparently sincere religious men who have been regular sexual abusers of children. This occurs within Christianity, Buddhism, Judaism, Islam and Hinduism. Because of the importance of religious belief and religious institutions in maintaining the unity of the social fabric, such activities have often been hidden ... In the Pakistani publication *Subha* it is claimed that the typical Islamic way of dealing with the subject of child prostitution is to contend that, since such practices were forbidden by religion and banned by law, they therefore do not exist.'[20]

To many commentators, consumers of the mass media are also a community of believers and much more influential in forming life values. How many children go to church, for example, and how many watch television? As long ago as the sixties, when John Lennon could say that the Beatles were 'more popular than Jesus', it was obvious where young people's view of sexuality was most likely to be formed. If we are to make a difference to the underlying values and attitudes that are at the very heart of commercial sexual exploitation of children, we must make sure that all the agents in the formation of values and attitudes find their own way to help in the fight.

The Foreign Minister of Belgium, arriving at the Stockholm Congress from a country still dazed by the events of late summer 1996 and the deaths of four young girls at the hands of sex exploiters, said,

> There is an analogy between the fight against sexual exploitation of children for commercial purposes and the fight against cancer. Even if we are able to localise and neutralise tumours, the illness still spreads around the planet and proliferates in the same way as metastases infiltrate and develop within the human body. Each organ, each continent, each country may be affected. The electronic information systems and the global communication networks are the blood vessels and the lymphatic system which allow child pornography and criminal activities to spread ... We need to combine our forces, our wills, our means and resources in order to neutralise the visible tumours of this cancer and to persecute and destroy their metastases before they develop into new tumours.

While we are still looking for ways to stop cancer taking hold and trying to find a cure, all over the world there are people who are taking a knife to existing cancers and cutting them out.

Programmes to combat exploitation

Sompop Jantraka began working in the north of Thailand in the late eighties to research the socio-economic effects of children being sold into prostitution. Another report, another indication that something needed to be done. Sompop Jantraka did that something. In 1989, he founded the Centre for Development and Education for Daughters and Communities, which soon became known as the Daughters Education Programme (DEP). The programme aimed to cut out the cancer at its roots, by tackling the way communities in northern Thailand looked at the value of their daughters. By helping girl-children to receive an education, Sompop reasoned, and by equipping them with vocational skills, his programme would increase their employment opportunities and thus their status.

The DEP centre is in Mai Sai district of Chiang Rai province, in the northernmost part of Thailand, on the border with Myanmar. This was not a random choice of location. The centre is at the very heart of cross-border trafficking in young girls from Myanmar and from the northern hill tribes into Bangkok. In the early years, Sompop raised most of his funding from wealthy Thais, and received a set-up grant from the Japanese Asian Children's Fund. By 1994, the programme was so successful and receiving so much favourable publicity that bigger donors moved in. UNICEF, the International Labour Organisation (ILO) and ECPAT contributed funds for five years, from 1994 to 1998, with UNICEF's contribution largely going to a leadership component in the programme which trains young women to manage the DEP project in their own villages.

In 1989, the DEP supported 19 girls of secondary school age. By 1996, 350 girls were benefiting from DEP support to go through primary, secondary school or vocational training. There are now centres in Huai So, Huai Khrai, Mae Suai, Wiangkaen and Phan, overseen by young women who have gone through the leadership programme, and supported also by parents and members of the community who have been drawn into the programme through counselling and advice on ways to increase their income.

At its simplest, DEP aims to help each girl through three years of secondary school, at least. DEP covers the costs of school fees, uniforms, equipment, medical treatment, transport and school activities. Usually the girls will attend the local school but, if there is none or if the girls are vulnerable at home, they are accommodated in DEP centres. The vocational training helps girls to learn gem-cutting, silver-work and sewing, and then helps them set up small businesses or find employment. Many of the girls, though, come through the programme with higher ambitions still, 'I would like to be a doctor,' one 11-year-old told a reporter.[21] 'I would like to come back and work at DEP, help kids who are sick.' Another 11-year-old girl was convinced of the value of the schooling she had received through DEP. 'I would like to be a leader and a community development worker,' she said. 'I would like to work up in the hills and have a school for children who have no school to go to.' These girls' desire to give back to their community the help they had received from DEP also illustrates another aspect of the work DEP does: it aims to help young girls to see the value of their culture and communities. In this way, the communities value the girls and the feeling is mutual. So successful has the programme been that the Thai Government is looking at using it as a model for similar centres throughout the country, and it is a model that could easily be used in other countries, including those in the industrialised world.

The self-help element built into the DEP is also strategically important, because children who have been caught in the sex trade and those who are vulnerable to exploiters are often marginalised from mainstream society and out of the loop of normal information networks and support mechanisms. Former prostituted children and young adults are therefore particularly effective workers in the campaign to stop commercial sexual exploitation of children. They are street-wise, credible and sensitive as no-one else can be to the realities of exploitation.

Alfredo, a healthy, swaggering 15-year-old, the kind most people would call 'a real character', spends the hours many kids would spend fooling around with friends and dodging homework on the streets of one of Brazil's biggest cities, trying to help street kids who might fall into the clutches of pimps and exploiters.[22] He finds it easy to talk to the kids and, more importantly, they find it easy to talk to him. They share the same tastes in music. They wear the same sort of baseball caps. They laugh at the same jokes. They were once in the same business. Alfredo sold sex on the streets to survive, as these kids do or might end up doing. When he talks to them, tells them how they can find work, where they can go for food and advice, what they should look out for and avoid, he is talking from personal experience, and it makes all the difference in the world to the kids who are listening to him.

'Employing people who have first-hand experience of this form of abuse and violence can go a long way to healing the hurt of present victims simply because they know that these people have had the same experience *and have come through it*. It can also nurture the return of self-esteem and dignity in the lives of past victims, by the discovery that other people need them.'[23]

In the same way that Alfredo can help young people because of his past experiences, adult prostitutes in Brazil use their experience of their current lives to encourage young girls who are vulnerable to commercial sexual exploitation to look for other options. In Cambodia, young girls rescued from brothels into which they had been sold travel into small communities acting out the fear and violence they suffered, as a warning not only to children who might fall into the same trap but also to parents who might not be aware of the dangers their children face if sold into bonded labour.

This quasi-educational task is extremely important in areas where the vulnerable child falls victim to exploitation through the ignorance of her parents. Education is consequently a vital element of the fight to stop sexual exploitation of children, not only for the children themselves, who find through formal education alternative ways to earn a living and greater strength to avoid vulnerability traps, but also for parents and, indeed, whole communities who simply may not recognise the dangers their children face. Education in the form of training is important, too, for police officers, customs officers, travel and tourism professionals, media representatives, health workers, social workers – in fact anyone who might cross the path between vulnerability and exploitation down which the child travels. UNICEF has been particularly active in supporting educational programmes, one of its traditional programming priorities, and has given support to the training of law enforcement personnel in South East Asia, to girls' education in Cambodia and Thailand, and to social awareness campaigns in Brazil.[24] Also, UNICEF has committed itself to integrating awareness of the vulnerability of some children to commercial sexual exploitation of children into the planning of its development programmes. One example is a project in Cambodia, Community Action for Social Development, which looks at ways of integrating the best interests of the child into all elements of the programme, for example by linking the criteria for credit facilities and income-generating opportunities with parents' care of their children. In other words, the better the parents care for their children, the more likely they are to receive loans and support in projects to generate income for their family.[25]

While education, development programmes, legal reform and awareness of the image of the child are all aimed at reducing the vulnerability of children and helping to prevent them from commercial sexual exploitation, work has also begun on looking at the clients of prostituted children and what can be done to prevent them from buying sex with minors.

For the clients, too, education is an important tool for change. Ignorance of the age of the child, of the immorality of buying sex with a child, and of the damaging long-term impact on the child, is no excuse for exploiting children. It has to and can be changed. At the Stockholm Congress[26] there were calls for preventative education programmes for prostitute users and potential prostitute users, to help them see that indiscriminately using under-age children when they are offered is wrong. At the same time, programmes can start to try to shift the popular but misplaced notion that men 'need' sex and so have a right to buy or take it when they see fit. This is an important message to get across to young people before they become sexually active, and it needs to be given to young women as well as young men. They need to understand the impact of sexual exploitation on children, the damage to their dignity, their health, their future. They should have some idea of why adult women become prostitutes, of laws governing sexual activity, including the age of consent, and how racism and gender bias work to put some women and children at risk of abuse.

There needs to be more work, too, with specific groups who have been shown to have exploiters in their midst in the past: the armed forces, UN and other international peace-keepers, business travellers, tourists, migrant workers, aid, youth and social workers, missionaries and church personnel. Julia O'Connell Davidson has described these groups as 'captive audiences', and the organisations or groupings to which they belong could easily take some responsibility for helping them to understand the issues involved in buying children for sex. There are many small non-governmental organisations, as well as larger organisations like ECPAT and UNICEF, which have been working in this field for some years now and which have the expertise and experience to pass on in training courses, briefings and discussion sessions. For some of these groups, publications have been prepared pointing out the risk situation into which the men are passing – tourists, for example, on planes or in customs areas – and there are ancillary actions that can be taken to target specific groups, for example agencies which fund social and youth projects in areas where children are trapped in prostitution should 'exercise great caution where a) the project is founded and run by a single foreign male and administered without accountability to the local community, and b) the project has as its sole focus assistance to poor young children'.[27]

Reporting and tracking the exploiters

Beyond prevention, much more could be done to improve the policing and reporting of those who sexually exploit children. National databases which register convicted sex offenders, mechanisms for sharing such information across state lines and, potentially, international borders, and media strategies which lead to public condemnation of offenders without hounding those whose guilt has not been proven (an important balance to keep to ensure fairness and reactions against 'witch-hunts') are some ways the decision-makers and opinion-formers in our societies can help.

A mechanism for speedily recording and circulating information on missing children – ideally running parallel to police reporting, not integrated into it – is also important. The UK-based National Missing Persons' Helpline is a good example of how well-collected data can be used to publicise missing persons, help trace and record their return as well as provide computer-aged photos of young children, all in an environment independent of the authorities and reassuring to families whose loved ones have gone missing. Yet, despite the six-year experience of the UK Helpline, by mid-1997 public anger at perceived government inaction in the Dutroux case in Belgium had resulted in the creation of a Brussels-based 'European Centre for Missing and

Exploited Children' on the model of the American National Centre for Missing and Exploited Children. A Paris-based 'European' centre was then announced for September 1997 and, in June 1997, a group of Americans proposed the creation of yet another 'European' centre to the Swiss Government. It is to be hoped that the lesson of Stockholm – cooperation, networking and collaboration – will have been learned and that these diverse projects will be at the very least fully compatible and lead to European cooperation and networking rather than a competitive free-for-all. If competition and lack of cooperation prevail, children will suffer.

Beyond national initiatives such as these, however, each member of civil society, can also play a part. How many people simply turn a blind eye to behaviour which they think seems suspicious? How many of us reassure ourselves that 'it could not happen here'? It should be fairly clear by now that it can, and does, happen just about everywhere, so that we all need to be alert and, while not automatically thinking the worst and certainly with no sense of witch-hunt, we should be ready to do something to intervene when we think a child is at risk. The hundreds of thousands of western tourists who pour into Asia each year, for example, are quite likely to see western men with young girls in bars and restaurants, or just walking down the street. Tourists might see western men on the beach openly fondling young children. At the very least, questions should be asked of this behaviour and local authorities, ECPAT or Save the Children or other child rights groups in the areas should be alerted. On a more formal scale, organisations responsible for groups of men who traditionally buy sex in the commercial sex market, and who might inadvertently or willingly seek out children as sex partners, should take responsibility for the actions of these men and make it clear that exploitative behaviour will not be tolerated.

Laws and law enforcement, media reporting and the image of the child, tourism charters and publicity, programmes in prevention, education, recovery, awareness of values and attitudes towards the child and, vitally, cooperation and networking in all initiatives undertaken – action is needed on all these fronts and for as long as it takes to fight against those who are selling and buying children for sex. With this in mind, delegates at the Stockholm Congress in August 1996 adopted a *Declaration and Agenda for Action*. The Agenda is a sort of check-list of the actions that different sectors can take as their contribution to the campaign to end commercial sexual exploitation of children and, in the closing days of the Congress, participants worked in small groups to begin to put into place the building blocks for national action plans which will bring together all the different players. 'When you return home, you must make the words of the Declaration and Agenda for Action come alive,' Queen Silvia of Sweden told delegates at the closing session of the Congress. 'We who are here today and many, many more are now part of a global network which includes governments and every sector of society.

We know that as long as there is any child who is being sexually exploited, there is work to do. We can never let our vision of what is possible be limited by what appear to be invincible obstacles. Much can be achieved in no time if there is commitment, dedication and cooperation.'[28]

The backdrop to these stirring calls to action and the toil of national planning is the words of the Stockholm Declaration:

> The World Congress reiterates its commitment to the rights of the child, bearing in mind the Convention on the Rights of the Child, and calls upon all states in cooperation with national and international organisations and civil society to:
> - accord high priority to action against the commercial sexual exploitation of children and allocate adequate resources for this purpose;
> - promote stronger cooperation between states and all sectors of society to prevent children from entering the sex trade and to strengthen the role of families in protecting children against commercial sexual exploitation;
> - criminalise the commercial sexual exploitation of children, as well as other forms of sexual exploitation of children, and condemn and penalise all those offenders involved, whether local or foreign, while ensuring that the child victims of this practice are not penalised;
> - review and revise, where appropriate, laws, policies, programmes and practices to eliminate the commercial sexual exploitation of children;
> - enforce laws, policies and programmes to protect children from commercial sexual exploitation and strengthen communication and cooperation between law enforcement authorities;
> - promote adoption, implementation and dissemination of laws, policies, and programmes supported by relevant regional, national and local mechanisms against the commercial sexual exploitation of children;
> - develop and implement comprehensive gender-sensitive plans and programmes to prevent the commercial sexual exploitation of children, to protect and assist the child victims and to facilitate their recovery and reintegration into society;
> - create a climate through education, social mobilisation, and development activities to ensure that parents and others legally responsible for children are able to fulfill their rights, duties and responsibilities to protect children from commercial sexual exploitation;
> - mobilise political and other partners, national and international communities, including intergovernmental organisations and non-governmental organisations, to assist countries in eliminating the commercial sexual exploitation of children; and
> - enhance the role of popular participation, including that of children, in preventing and eliminating the commercial sexual exploitation of children.[29]

The Stockholm Congress set target deadlines for two specific actions: 'by the year 2000, the Agenda for Action calls for strong, comprehensive, cross-sectoral, integrated strategies and measures to be moulded into national agendas for action, with indicators of progress, set goals and time-frames; by the year 2000, the Agenda for Action calls for development of databases on vulnerable children and their exploiters, with relevant research and disaggregated data'.[30] These deadlines allow only four years between the Congress and the time for reckoning when the whole world, mobilised by NGOs and press into a global monitoring body for the promises made in Stockholm, will ask what progress has been made.

The dawn of a new millennium

Writing in 1994, Ron O'Grady, International Co-ordinator of ECPAT, the campaign that has done so much to alert the world to the horrors of children forced into the sex trade, looked forward to 1996 and expressed the hope that, by that time, the world would be 'on the way to ending this modern slavery of children'.[31] The Stockholm Congress was a clear signal that the world is, indeed, on that path. But O'Grady also had in mind a turn of century deadline: 'let us hope that at least by the year 2000 we can find a solution,' he wrote. 'It would help to give us a little more meaning to our entry into the 21st century – into the future – if we could feel that we have found a way to protect the future of humanity by the obvious but necessary step of protecting our own children.'

It is 31 December 1999. A young child is walking home from school in a small town in central Europe. A car pulls into the kerb and crawls alongside her. The driver leans out of the window and calls to her, 'Hello. Are you going home? You're going to get wet, you know, it's going to rain. Why don't you come and let me take you home?' Across the road, a woman cleaning her windows sees the child and the man in the car calling to her. She notes his number, calls the police and runs out into the street. 'Are you on your way home dear? I'll walk with you until a policeman comes to make sure you get home safely.' The car speeds away. Meanwhile, in the local police station, a keystroke at the computer has called up the car registration number and checked it against a list of convicted sex offenders known to reside in the general area. The car belongs to a man in his mid-thirties who spent two years in jail in another European country for molesting a child in a park. An hour later, the man has been taken for questioning and for a preliminary meeting with a psychologist who specialises in sex crimes and preventative treatment of potential offenders. The young girl is at home, safe.

Meanwhile, on the other side of the world, it is midday in a great Asian metropolis. Police officers, customs officers, child rights workers, a group of television journalists and a lobby group representing families from a small community in a neighbouring country are meeting to finalise plans to move in on a brothel in the downtown area where tourists have reported touts who have offered them young children for sex. The tourists have made sworn statements to the police and to their diplomatic embassies in the country. Two hours later, members of the child rights and lobby groups have infiltrated the brothel disguised as customers. When the police and TV cameras move in, they block the exits and stop the pimps and exploiters from escaping. The two young children found cowering in a small cubicle at the back of the brothel are swept up in the arms of a specially trained children's officer. They will be given food, counselling and sympathy while they are awaiting the arrival of their families, who reported them missing. The exploiters will face harsh penalties and the customers of the adult prostitutes' brothel will be obliged to undergo counselling and awareness-raising training to discourage them from ever considering paying for sex with children. The footage shot by the television crew will be kept safe to be used as evidence before being shown on the evening news and made available to child rights organisations to use in awareness-raising videos for vulnerable communities.

In a South American beach resort, a well-dressed woman arrives at her hotel with a young boy in tow. She requests her room key from the desk clerk. 'I'm sorry, madam,' the clerk says, 'but guests are not allowed in the rooms at any time.' The woman takes out her purse and slides a $50 bill across the counter. 'This is the son of a friend of mine in town,' she says. 'He's just going to keep me company until his uncle fetches him later.' The clerk slides the money back towards the woman. 'I'm very sorry,' he says, never losing his professional smile, 'but the hotel has strict rules on this. There is a comfortable sitting area just across the hallway, where you and your guest can drink tea and watch the television. May I suggest you wait there?'

Julie Lejeune and Mélissa Russo. Daniel Handley. Rosario Baluyot. Four young children whose lives were cut short for the sake of illicit sexual pleasure. Four young children whose deaths must galvanise us into action so that, when the new millennium dawns, all the children of our world will be safe from the men and women who kidnap, drug, steal, force, abuse, exploit, torture and sell children for sex.

Notes

Chapter 1

1   In the closing press conference at the first World Congress against Commercial Sexual Exploitation of Children, held in Stockholm, Sweden, 27–31 August 1996.
2   Survey undertaken by the non-governmental organisation CARE Cambodia in 1994.
3   *Sex Tourism in Thailand*, research paper by Julia O'Connell Davidson and Jacqueline Sanchez Taylor, UK 1994, published by ECPAT 1996.
4   *The Sex Exploiter*, Julia O'Connell Davidson, ECPAT, May 1996.
5   'Kids for sale', Bob Herbert, *The New York Times*, 22 January 1996.
6   *Sex, money and morality: Prostitution and tourism in Southeast Asia*, T. Truong, Zed Books, London 1990, p.199.
7   *Sex Tourism in Thailand*, op.cit., p.4.
8   In late 1996 ECPAT International, recognising that its work had spread from Asia into other parts of the world, dropped the Asia-based definition of its acronym and began simply using the name ECPAT without defining it. Some national ECPAT members do, however, use the definition 'End Child Prostitution, Pornography and Trafficking'.
9   'The Carnal Cabaret', J. Illman, *The Guardian*, 30 November 1993.
10 'Asia's plantations of the '90s', Nicholas D. Kristof, *International Herald Tribune*, 15 April 1996.
11 The names of children who are still alive have been changed to protect their identity. The names of exploiters have not.
12 The young woman here called Son Ma agreed to this interview during the shooting of a UNICEF video on child trafficking and prostitution in Cambodia.
13 'Virgin Territory', *The Economist*, 2 March 1996.
14 'Nepal: the child sex trade', Sue Lloyd-Roberts, *Insight News Television*, 1995.
15 *Back home from the brothels*, Gauri Pradhan, Child Workers in Nepal Concerned Centre, August 1996.
16 'Cross border threat', *India Today*, March 1994.
17 Report from Reynaldo Bulgarelli, UNICEF officer in Brazil.
18 Report of the Council of Women's Rights, Ceara Brazil, quoted by Agence France Presse, 7 March 1996.

19   Report of the Centre for Reference, Studies and Action for Children and Adoles-
     cents (CECRIA), April 1996, quoted by Agence France Presse, 12 April 1996.
20   Report in *Le Nouveau Quotidien*, 13 October 1993.
21   *Child prostitution and sex tourism in Costa Rica*, Julia O'Connell Davidson and
     Jacqueline Sanchez Taylor, ECPAT 1996.
22   Interviewed by O'Connell Davidson and Sanchez Taylor, who did not give the
     real names of the men they interviewed.
23   There has never been any suggestion Mr Hawke or, indeed, any of the patrons of
     The Refuge were aware of the events that are described here, and it is not
     intended in any way to suggest that they were implicated in these events.
24   'Paedophiles spawn tragic legacy', *The Bulletin*, 9 April 1996.
25   'Out of the shadows', *Newsweek*, 6 May 1996.
26   'Swedish politician has Thai wife, 14', *Bangkok Post*, 10 January 1996.
27   'Abus sexuels et mensonges' (Sexual abuse and lies), *Le Nouveau Quotidien*, 4
     November 1996.
28   'Dawn Shields was a smiling 15-year-old . . .', *The Guardian*, 12 February 1996.
29   'Une scandale de prostitution enfantine secoue Séville' (A child prostitution
     scandal shakes Seville), *Libération*, 7 February 1996.
30   *L'enfant du Bois de Boulogne*, Collection Les Enfants du Fleuve, Fayard 1989.
31   'Ceausescu's orphans', *Time*, 24 June 1996.
32   *Commercial sexual exploitation of children in some Eastern European countries*, Helena
     Karlen and Christina Hagner, ECPAT, March 1996, p.14.

Chapter 2

1   *Opening session statement for the World Congress against Commercial Sexual Exploita-
     tion of Children*, Laurie Robinson, Assistant Attorney General, Office of Justice
     Programs, US Department of Justice, 27 August 1996.
2   'Spooked by abuse', *The Wall Street Journal*, 13 September 1996.
3   'Nightmare on any street', Owen Bowcott and Erlend Clouston, *The Guardian*, 6
     June 1997.
4   Figure based on a survey by the US arm of Defence for Children International,
     and quoted by UNICEF in the Press Kit for the World Congress against Commer-
     cial Sexual Exploitation of Children.
5   'In Chicago, it's coffee and condoms for runaway kids', Danielle Bochove,
     Reuters, reprinted in *The Nation*, 25 December 1995.
6   Ibid.
7   'Prostitution's sickening trade in children', *Reader's Digest*, August 1994.
8   Kimberley Gamble-Payne, quoted in the *ECPAT Australia Newsletter*, August
     1996.
9   National Criminal Investigation Division, Ministry of the Interior, Angola.
10   *Message from President Nelson Mandela* to the World Congress against Commercial
     Sexual Exploitation of Children, 27 August 1996.
11   'Hope for Johannesburg brothel kids', Robyn Green for Reuters, *The Geneva Post*,
     4 May 1995.
12   Report by Agence France Presse, 27 July 1995.
13   Julia O'Connell Davidson and Jacqueline Sanchez Taylor, whose report for
     ECPAT gave the details on which this section is based, indicate that the use of the
     terms 'white, black and coloured' do not in any way endorse the idea of race 'as a

biological fact' but reflect the 'social categories used in South Africa to structure inequalities and organise social relations'.

14   'Child prostitution drawing tourists', *Associated Press*, 21 November 1995.
15   'On Nairobi's streets, teenage prostitutes offer evidence of a world gone awry', *International Herald Tribune*, 3 January 1991.
16   'Zyira is raped every week', Caroline Lees, *The Sunday Express*, 25 August 1996.
17   *An end to silence: a preliminary study on sexual violence, abuse and exploitation of children affected by armed conflict*, Eylah Kadjar-Hamouda for the UN Study on the impact of armed conflict on children (the 'Machel study'), November 1996.
18   *Child prostitution, a case study in military camps in Liberia*, Anita Bevan, Save the Children Fund 1996.
19   *Experiences with regard to the United Nations peace-keeping forces in Mozambique*, Redd Barna 1995.
20   *The child and the tourist*, Ron O'Grady, ECPAT 1992.
21   1 Kings, v2.
22   'Domestics in Middle East face widespread exploitation, abuse', Edward Yeranian, *Christian Science Monitor*, 6 May 1997.
23   *Early marriage*, Anti-Slavery International, Geneva 1994.
24   'America's child brides', *Marie Claire Australia*, January 1996.
25   *National legislation and international trafficking in child pornography*, Laura J. Lederer, Centre on Speech, Equality and Harm, University of Minnesota 1996.

Chapter 3

1   *Sexual Exploitation of Children*, Study series No. 8, United Nations Centre for Human Rights, May 1996.
2   'Who on earth would allow a child of 12 to pose like this?', Geoffrey Levy, *Daily Mail*, 7 May 1996.
3   *Prime time for children: media, ethics and the reporting of commercial sexual exploitation*, Kate Holman and Aidan White, International Federation of Journalists, for UNICEF, May 1996.
4   Ibid.
5   Quoted in *Female* magazine, October 1996.
6   This term for a long Russian literary tradition of young women discovering sexuality is borrowed from Nina Berberova, *Nabokov et sa Lolita*, Actes Sud 1996.
7   'Hollywood Lolitas: the scandal of the teenage seductress', *Marie Claire*, May 1996.
8   'Affaire de pédophilie en France' (A paedophile affair in France), *Agence France Presse*, 9 November 1996.
9   *Introductory statement to Media Panel participants*, Stockholm Congress, 29 August 1996.
10   *National legislation and international trafficking in child pornography*, op.cit.
11   *Commercial child pornography in Sweden: silenced knowledge and obscured oppression*, Folkaktionen mot Pornografi, Stockholm 1996.
12   'Child pornography still a problem in Sweden: experts', *Bangkok Post*, 8 January 1996.
13   Privacy and paedophilia, *The Economist*, 3 August 1996.
14   *Commercial child pornography in Sweden*, op.cit., p.24.
15   As of June 1997, only two countries have not signed: Somalia and the United States.

16　'Fathers sell daughters to shame and fantasy', Derek Brown, *The Guardian*, 4 November 1992.

17　*Trafficking of children and prostitution*, Richard Young and Helen Chernikoff, UNICEF India Country Office, February 1996.

18　'Child slaves "used by West Africans to appease spirits"', Sam Kiley, *The Times*, 17 September 1996.

19　*The forgotten girl-slaves of West Africa*, Paul Bravender-Coyle, The Anti-Slavery Society, 1996.

20　*The Nation*, Thailand, 14 November 1995; *Philippine Daily Enquirer*, 3 January 1996; *Manila Times*, 29 January 1996; *Bangkok Post*, 22 February 1996; *The Nation*, 27 February 1996; *Le Monde*, 26 May 1996; *Le Figaro*, 9 May 1996.

21　*Child pornography: an international perspective*, Peggy Healy for ECPAT, May 1996.

22　AFP Report, 13 May 1997.

23　'CompuServe's censorship list claim denied', *Bangkok Post*, 4 January 1996.

24　'CompuServe lifts sex ban', *Bangkok Post*, 22 February 1996.

25　'CompuServe will allow sex chats', *The Nation*, 27 February 1996.

26　Report from Agence France Presse, 8 May 1996.

27　'Pornographie enfantine sur Internet' (Child pornography on the Internet), *Tribune de Genève*, 12 December 1996.

28　'Child pornography in the computer age', Ron O'Grady, speech given at the Asian Regional Consultation for the World Congress against Commercial Sexual Exploitation of Children, Bangkok, April 1996.

29　'Priest led Internet paedophile ring', *The Guardian*, 13 November 1996.

Chapter 4

1　'Priest tracks down child sex suspect who jumped bail', *The Times*, 31 August 1996.

2　*The sex exploiter*, op.cit.

3　'A sex lesson too far', *The Guardian*, 21 February 1996.

4　Ibid.

5　*The commercial sexual exploitation of street children*, World Vision, July 1996, p.30.

6　*The child and the tourist*, op.cit., p.68.

7　*The sex exploiter*, op.cit., p.20.

8　*La prunelle de mes yeux (The pupil of my eyes)*, Gabriel Matzneff, Gallimard 1993, p.300.

9　Ibid., p.332.

10　Ibid, p.173.

11　*Mes amours décomposés (My decomposed loves)*, Gabriel Matzneff, Gallimard-Folio, Paris 1992.

12　'Un projet de loi prévoit le renforcement de la répression des abus sexuels sur les enfants' (Law project to reinforce repression of sexual abuse of children), *Le Monde*, 21 November 1996.

13　'Sex offenders face tagging', *The Guardian*, 18 June 1996.

14　'Le procès de Spartacus' (The Spartacus trial), *Le Figaro*, 16 February 1995; 'L'éditeur du guide Spartacus sera jugé en Belgique'(Editor of Spartacus guide to be judged in Belgium), *Journal de Genève*, 16 November 1994; 'Le pasteur anglican et la pédophilie internationale' (The Anglican priest and international paedophilia), *Le Monde*, 24 November 1994, 'L'enfer de la pédophilie sans frontières' (Paedophile hell has no boundaries), *Le Figaro*, 22 November 1994.

15 The *Guide* is still being published, albeit in a version which claims to be 'expurgated'. Researchers insist, however, that they are able to find in it and decode information usable by those seeking children for sex.
16 'Evil in paradise', Martin Cottingham, *The Tablet*, 19 October 1996.
17 Ibid. Thanks to the people at Christian Aid for their help.
18 'Fitzgerald sentenced to minimum of 8 years', *The Nation*, 8 May 1996; 'Child sex sailor, 66, jailed for 17 years', *The Age*, 8 May 1996; 'A wrenching way to jail an abuser', *Christian Science Monitor*, August 1996.
19 'The Paedo File', *ECPAT Newsletter*, No. 17, August 1996.
20 *The child and the tourist*, op.cit., p.21.
21 *The child and the tourist*, op.cit., p.30.
22 Editorial, *Philippines Daily Enquirer*, 22 December 1987.
23 *Sex tourism and child prostitution in the Dominican Republic*, Julia O'Connell Davidson and Jacqueline Sanchez Taylor, ECPAT 1996, pp.18–19.
24 'Buying sex in a different currency', *The Nation*, 28 July 1991, quoted in *The child and the tourist*, op.cit.
25 *Sex tourism and child prostitution in the Dominican Republic*, op.cit., p.27.
26 *Sex tourism and child prostitution in South Africa*, Julia O'Connell Davidson and Jacqueline Sanchez Taylor, ECPAT 1996, pp.18–19.
27 *Child prostitution and sex tourism in Costa Rica*, op.cit., pp.24–25.
28 *The child and the tourist*, op.cit., p.78.
29 *Sydney Morning Herald*, 14–24 May 1996, quoted in *ECPAT News*, ECPAT Australia.
30 Anita Gradin, statement to the World Congress against Commercial Sexual Exploitation of Children, August 1996.
31 *Preliminary report on regional child trafficking and prostitution*, Centre for Protection of Children's Rights (CPCR) and Foundation for Children (FFC) for UNICEF East Asia and Pacific Regional Office, Bangkok, October 1995.
32 *The child and the tourist*, op.cit., pp.138–139.
33 *Factsheet 13: Trafficking routes*, World Congress against Commercial Sexual Exploitation of Children, June 1996.
34 Jose Ayala Lasso, former United Nations High Commissioner for Human Rights, keynote speech to the World Congress against Commercial Sexual Exploitation of Children, 27 August 1996.
35 'The role of customs in monitoring pornography', paper prepared for the *Enforcing the law against the commercial sexual exploitation of children* consultation, Bangkok, January 1996.
36 All the keynote speeches from the World Congress against Commercial Sexual Exploitation of Children can be found at the Congress World Wide Web site. Its Internet address is: http://www.childhub.ch/webpub/csechome. ECPAT also has a home page on the Internet, at: http://www.rb.se/ecpat.

Chapter 5

1 'Convention on the Rights of the Child: a message about ethics, an instrument for change', Thomas Hammarberg, *News on Health Care in Developing Countries*, Vol. 10, February 1996.
2 *The international legal framework and current national legislative and enforcement responses*, Muireann O'Briain for ECPAT, August 1996.
3 'Europol joins child sex battle', *The European*, 5 December 1996.

4   Act 97/154/JHA, *Official Journal of the European Communities*, Vol. 40, 4 March 1997.
5   'Extraterritorial law in France', Juristes du Monde, *Enforcing the law against the commercial sexual exploitation of children (Bangkok Consultation)*, ECPAT, January 1996.
6   'Prosecuting child sex tourists at home', Peggy Healy, *Bangkok Consultation*, ECPAT 1996.
7   'Child prostitution: challenging law enforcement towards the year 2000', Ann Kristin-Olsen, Chairperson of the Interpol Standing Working Party on Offences against Minors, *Bangkok Consultation*, ECPAT 1996.
8   *Factsheet 9: Legal Protection*, World Congress against Commercial Sexual Exploitation of Children, 1996.
9   *Child sexual exploitation: improving investigations and protecting victims – a blueprint for action*, Office for Victims of Crime, US Department of Justice, January 1995.
10 *Measures taken by the Royal Thai Government to combat child prostitution in Thailand*, Fact sheet, 19 March 1996.
11 *Rapporteur's summary of Panel 3b: The role of the media*, World Congress against Commercial Sexual Exploitation of Children, Stockholm, 30 August 1996.
12 Ibid.
13 *Keynote address* by Carol Bellamy, Executive Director of the United Nations Children's Fund, UNICEF, to the World Congress against Commercial Sexual Exploitation of Children, Stockholm, 27 August 1996.
14 *Panel 3b: Rapporteur's summary*, op.cit.
15 *Female* magazine, October 1996.
16 *Statement to the World Congress against Commercial Sexual Exploitation of Children*, Marta Santos Pais, Rapporteur for the UN Committee on the Rights of the Child, August 1996.
17 *Tourism and children in prostitution*, Martin Staebler for ECPAT, May 1996.
18 *The child and the tourist*, op.cit., p.61.
19 *The rape of the innocent*, Ron O'Grady, ECPAT 1994, p.118.
20 Ibid., pp.116–117.
21 'Providing an alternative to prostitution for Thailand's hill tribe children', *AIDS Analysis Asia*, Vol. 2 (2), March 1996, pp.6–7.
22 Youth delegation press conference, Stockholm Congress, 31 August 1996.
23 *Children and prostitution*, Florence Bruce, International Catholic Child Bureau, Geneva 1996, p.47.
24 *Statement at the hearing on the international exploitation of children, before the US Congressional Human Rights Caucus*, Bertil Lindblad, Senior Adviser, UNICEF, Washington DC, 22 May 1996, p.4.
25 *Panel 2a: Prevention and psychosocial rehabilitation, Rapporteur's summary*, Stockholm 1996.
26 *The sex exploiter*, op.cit.
27 *The sex exploiter*, op.cit., p.25.
28 *Closing address* of HM Queen Silvia of Sweden, World Congress against Commercial Sexual Exploitation of Children, Stockholm 1996.
29 *Declaration and Agenda for Action*, World Congress against Commercial Sexual Exploitation of Children, Stockholm 1996.
30 *Summary of the Final Report of the General Rapporteur*, UNICEF, September 1996.
31 *The child and the tourist*, op.cit., p.10.

Bibliography

Sources cited in the text

Alexis — *L'enfant du Bois de Boulogne*, Fayard, Paris 1989

Anti-Slavery International — *Early marriage*, Anti-Slavery International 1994

Berberova, N — *Nabokov et sa Lolita*, Actes Sud, Arles 1996

Best, S — 'The role of customs in monitoring pornography', *Enforcing the law against the commercial sexual exploitation of children* consultation (Bangkok), ECPAT 1996

Bevan, A — *Child prostitution, a case study in military camps in Liberia*, Save the Children Fund 1996

Bochove, D — 'In Chicago, it's coffee and condoms for runaway kids', *The Nation*, 25 December 1995

Bowcott, O and Clouston, E — 'Nightmare on any street', *The Guardian*, 6 June 1997

Bravender-Coyle, P — *The forgotten girl-slaves of West Africa*, Anti-Slavery Society 1996

Brown, D — 'Fathers sell daughters to shame and fantasy', *The Guardian*, 4 November 1992

Bruce, F — *Children and prostitution*, International Catholic Child Bureau 1996

Centre for Protection of Children's Rights — *Preliminary report on regional child trafficking and prostitution*, UNICEF East Asia and Pacific Regional Office 1995

137

Cottingham, M	'Evil in Paradise', *The Tablet*, 19 October 1996
ECPAT	'The Paedo File', *ECPAT Newsletter* No.17, August 1996
Folkaktionen mot Pornografi	*Commercial child pornography in Sweden: silenced knowledge and obscured oppression*, Folkaktionen mot Pornografi 1996
Green, R	'Hope for Johannesburg brothel kids', *The Geneva Post*, 4 May 1995
Hammarberg, T	'Convention on the Rights of the Child: a message about ethics, an instrument for change', *News on Health Care in Developing Countries*, Vol.10, February 1996
Healy, P (M)	*Child pornography: an international perspective*, ECPAT 1996
Healy, P (M)	'Prosecuting child sex tourists at home', *Enforcing the law against the commercial sexual exploitation of children* consultation (Bangkok), ECPAT 1996
Herbert, R	'Kids for sale', *New York Times*, 22 January 1996
Holman, K and White, A	*Prime time for children: media, ethics and the reporting of commercial sexual exploitation*, International Federation of Journalists/ UNICEF 1996
Illman, J	'The carnal cabaret', *The Guardian*, 30 November 1993
Juristes du Monde	'Extraterritorial law in France', *Enforcing the law against the commercial sexual exploitation of children* consultation (Bangkok), ECPAT 1996
Kadjar-Hamouda, E	*An end to silence: a preliminary study on sexual violence, abuse and exploitation of children affected by armed conflict*, NGO Group for the Convention on the Rights of the Child 1996
Karlen, H and Hagner, C	*Commercial sexual exploitation of children in some Eastern European countries*, ECPAT 1996
Kiley, S	'Child slaves used by West Africans to appease spirits', *The Times*, 17 September 1996

Kristin-Olsen, A 'Child prostitution: challenging law enforcement towards the year 2000', *Enforcing the law against the commercial sexual exploitation of children* consultation (Bangkok), ECPAT 1996

Kristof, N 'Asia's plantations of the '90s', *International Herald Tribune*, 15 April 1996

Lederer, L *National legislation and international trafficking in child pornography*, Centre on Speech, Equality and Harm, University of Minnesota 1996

Lees, C 'Zyira is raped every week', *Sunday Express*, 25 August 1996

Levy, G 'Who on earth would allow a child of 12 to pose like this?', *Daily Mail*, 7 May 1996

Lloyd Roberts, S 'Nepal: the child sex trade', *Insight News Television*, 1995

Matzneff, G *La prunelle de mes yeux*, Gallimard, Paris 1993

Matzneff, G *Mes amours décomposés*, Gallimard-Folio, Paris 1992

Muntarbhorn, V *Sexual exploitation of children*, Study series No.8, United Nations Centre for Human Rights 1996

O'Briain, M *The international legal framework and current national legislative and enforcement responses*, ECPAT 1996

O'Connell Davidson, J *The sex exploiter*, ECPAT 1996

O'Connell Davidson, J and Sanchez Taylor, J *Child prostitution and sex tourism in Costa Rica*, ECPAT 1996

O'Connell Davidson, J and Sanchez Taylor, J *Sex tourism and child prostitution in the Dominican Republic*, ECPAT 1996

O'Connell Davidson, J and Sanchez Taylor, J *Sex tourism and child prostitution in South Africa*, ECPAT 1996

O'Connell Davidson, J and Sanchez Taylor, J *Sex tourism in Thailand*, ECPAT 1996

O'Grady, R 'Child pornography in the computer age', speech to *Asian Regional consultation for the World Congress against Commercial Sexual Exploitation of Children* (Bangkok) 1996

O'Grady, R *The child and the tourist*, ECPAT 1992

O'Grady, R *The rape of the innocent*, ECPAT 1994

Pradhan, G — *Back home from the brothels*, Child Workers in Nepal Concerned Centre 1996

Schade, E — *Experiences with regard to the United Nations peace-keeping forces in Mozambique*, Redd Barna 1995

Staebler, M — *Tourism and children in prostitution*, ECPAT 1996

Truong, T — *Sex, money and morality: Prostitution and tourism in Southeast Asia*, Zed Books, London 1990

United States Department of Justice — *Child sexual exploitation: improving investigations and protecting victims – a blueprint for action*, US Department of Justice 1995

World Vision — *The commercial sexual exploitation of street children*, World Vision 1996

Yeranian, E — 'Domestics in Middle East face widespread exploitation, abuse', *Christian Science Monitor*, 6 May 1997

Young, R and Chernikoff, H — *Trafficking of children and prostitution*, UNICEF India Country Office 1996

Newspaper articles

'Abus sexuels et mensonge', *Le Nouveau Quotidien*, 4 November 1996

'Affaire dé pedophilie en France', *Agence France Presse*, 9 November 1996

'America's child brides', *Marie Claire Australia*, January 1996

'Buying sex in a different currency', *The Nation*, 28 July 1991

'Child prostitution drawing tourists', *Associated Press*, 21 November 1995

'Ceausescu's orphans', *Time*, 24 June 1996

'Child pornography still a problem in Sweden: experts', *Bangkok Post*, 8 January 1996

'Child sex sailor, 66, jailed for 17 years', *The Age*, 8 May 1996

'CompuServe's censorship list claim denied', *Bangkok Post*, 4 January 1996

'CompuServe lifts sex ban', *Bangkok Post*, 22 February 1996

'CompuServe will allow sex chats', *The Nation*, 27 February 1996

'Cross border threat', *India Today*, March 1994

'Dawn shields was a smiling 15-year-old', *The Guardian*, 12 February 1996

'Europol joins child sex battle', *The European*, 5 December 1996

'Fitzgerald sentenced to minimum of 8 years', *The Nation*, 8 May 1996

'Hollywood Lolitas: the scandal of the teenage seductress', *Marie Claire*, May 1996

'L'éditeur du guide Spartacus sera jugé en Belgique', *Journal de Genève*, 16 November 1994

'L'enfer de la pédophilie sans frontières', *Le Figaro*, 22 November 1994

'Le pasteur anglican et la pédophilie internationale', *Le Monde*, 24 November 1994

'Le procés de Spartacus', *Le Figaro*, 16 February 1995

'On Nairobi's streets, teenage prostitutes offer evidence of a world gone awry', *International Herald Tribune*, 3 January 1991

'Out of the shadows', *Newsweek*, 6 May 1996

'Paedophiles spawn tragic legacy', *The Bulletin*, 9 April 1996

'Pornographie enfantine sur Internet', *Tribune de Genève*, 12 December 1996

'Priest led Internet paedophile ring', *The Guardian*, 13 November 1996

'Priest tracks down child sex suspect who jumped bail', *The Times*, 31 August 1996

'Privacy and paedophilia', *The Economist*, 3 August 1996

'Prostitution's sickening trade in children', *Reader's Digest*, August 1994

'Providing an alternative to prostitution

for Thailand's hill tribe children', *AIDS Analysis Asia* Vol.2(2), March 1996.

'A sex lesson too far', *The Guardian*, 21 February 1996

'Sex offenders face tagging', *The Guardian*, 18 June 1996

'Spooked by abuse', *The Wall Street Journal*, 13 September 1996

'Swedish politician has Thai wife, 14', *Bangkok Post*, 10 January 1996

'Une scandale de prostitution enfantine secoue Séville', *Liberation*, 7 February 1996

'Un projet de loi prévoit le renforcement de la répression des abus sexuels sur les enfants', *Le Monde*, 21 November 1996

'Virgin territory', *The Economist*, 2 March 1996

'A wrenching way to jail an abuser', *Christian Science Monitor*, August 1996

Documents from the World Congress against Commercial Sexual Exploitation of Children

Congress Web site at http://www.childhub.ch/webpub/csechome, including:
Factsheets on commercial sexual exploitation of children
Press kit of the World Congress
Theme working papers for the World Congress
Keynote speeches
Declaration and Agenda for Action

Report of the World Congress (Part I), Stockholm 1996, including:
Declaration and Agenda for Action
Opening statement by the Prime Minister of Sweden
Keynote speeches by the co-organisers
Other keynote speeches
Reports from the panels, workshops and regional dialogues
Concluding remarks by the General Rapporteur

Report of the World Congress (Part II), Stockholm 1996, including:
Statements by Heads of Delegation

Selected works not cited in the text

Axelsson, M — *Rosario is dead*, Raben Prisma, Sweden 1996

Bassiouni, M and McCormick, M — *Sexual violence: an invisible weapon of war in the Former Yugoslavia*, De Paul University 1996

Boonpala, P — *Strategy and action against the commercial sexual exploitation of children*, International Labour Office 1996

Bruce, F — *The sexual exploitation of children: field responses*, International Catholic Child Bureau 1991

Council of Europe — *Sexual exploitation, pornography and prostitution of, and trafficking in, children and young adults*, Council of Europe 1993

Dawant, R-P — *Marc Dutroux: Le dossier*, Editions Luc Pire, Brussels 1997

Ennew, J *et al.* — *Children and prostitution: how can we measure and monitor the commercial sexual exploitation of children?*, Centre for Family Research UK and Childwatch International Oslo 1996

Government of Romania — *Sexual exploitation and abuse of children*, Romanian National Child Protection Committee August 1996

Kalisz, S and Moriau, P — *Les cahiers d'un commissaire*, Editions Luc Pire, Brussels 1997

Nabokov, V — *Lolita*, Penguin Books, London 1995

NCH Action for Children — *Children on the Internet: a parent's guide*, NCH Action for Children December 1996

National Society for the Prevention of Cruelty to Children — *Protecting children from sexual abuse in the community: a guide for parents and carers*, NSPCC February 1997

Network against Child Labour — *Child prostitution in South Africa: a search for legal protection*, Network against Child Labour March 1996

Nyman, A and Svensson, B — *Boys: sexual abuse and treatment*, Radda Barnen 1995

O'Dea, P — *Gender exploitation and violence: the market in women, girls and sex in Nepal*, UNICEF 1993

Perio, G and Thierry, D — *Tourisme sexuel au Brésil et en Colombie,* Brussels 1996

Radda Barnen — *Rehabilitation of sexually abused children,* Radda Barnen (no date)

Svedin, C and Back K — *Children who don't speak out,* Radda Barnen 1996

Taliercio, C — *International law and legal aspects of child sex tourism in Asia,* Children's Ombudsman, Sweden 1996

O'Grady, R — *The ECPAT Story,* ECPAT 1996

UK Home Office — *Action against the commercial sexual exploitation of children: report by the Government of the United Kingdom,* UK Home Office August 1996

UN High Commissioner for Refugees — *Sexual violence against refugees,* UNHCR 1995

US Department of Labor — *Forced labor: the prostitution of children,* US Department of Labor 1996

Warburton, J and Camacho de la Cruz, M-T — *A right to happiness: approaches to the prevention and psycho-social recovery of child victims of commercial sexual exploitation,* NGO Group for the Convention on the Rights of the Child 1996